Warrior • 86

Boer Commando
1876–1902

Ian Knight • Illustrated by Raffaele Ruggeri

First published in Great Britain in 2004 by Osprey Publishing,
Midland House, West Way, Botley, Oxford OX2 0PH, UK
44-02 23rd St, Suite 219, Long Island City, NY 11101, USA
E-mail: info@ospreypublishing.com

Transferred to digital print on demand 2010

First published 2004
1st impression 2004

Printed and bound by PrintOnDemand-Worldwide.com, Peterborough, UK

A CIP catalogue record for this book is available from the British Library

ISBN: 978 1 84176 648 5

Editorial by Gerard Barker
Design by Ken Vail Graphic Design, Cambridge, UK
Index by Alan Thatcher
Originated by Grasmere Digital Imaging, Leeds, UK

Artist's note

Readers may care to note that the original paintings from which the colour plates in this book were prepared are available for
private sale. All reproduction copyright whatsoever is retained by the Publishers. All enquiries should be addressed to:
Raffaele Ruggeri
Via Indipendenza 22
Bologna
40121
Italy
The Publishers regret that they can enter into no correspondence upon this matter.

Author's Acknowledgements

My thanks to Ian Castle, who pointed me in the direction of a number of references regarding the 1881 campaign, to Ron Sheeley,
who kindly allowed me access to his picture collection, to Mark Siebenallar for his analysis of the weapons of the 1870s and 1880s,
and to Bill Cainan for access to his firearms collection. Pictures without a credit are from my private collection.

FOR A CATALOGUE OF ALL BOOKS PUBLISHED BY OSPREY
MILITARY AND AVIATION PLEASE CONTACT:

Osprey Direct, c/o Random House Distribution Center,
400 Hahn Road, Westminster, MD 21157
Email: uscustomerservice@ospreypublishing.com

Osprey Direct, The Book Service Ltd, Distribution Centre,
Colchester Road, Frating Green, Colchester, Essex, CO7 7DW
E-mail: customerservice@ospreypublishing.com

www.ospreypublishing.com

CONTENTS

BOER COMMANDO 1876–1902

INTRODUCTION

On the morning of 28 January 1881, Johannes de Bruyn, a 17-year-old farmer's son from the district of Heidelburg in the South African Republic (SAR), found himself in battle for the first time. Huddled against a line of low boulders piled up in front of a shallow shelter-trench, Johannes witnessed a sight which – despite years of conflict to come – would prove to be one of the most extraordinary of his life. Johannes' position lay on top of a ridge flanking the steep slope of the Laing's Nek pass, the border between the British colony of Natal and the Republic. At that moment, the positions on the pass were under a determined British attack. In front of Johannes, the ground fell away in a gentle slope for perhaps 80 yards before dropping into a steep valley beyond. A column of British infantry, struggling up from the valley, had just crested the rise and come into view; Johannes watched mesmerised as they hurried to deploy into line for their final attack. Their officers ran out in front, calling on the men to spread out, but the soldiers were tired from the climb, and their deployment was clumsy. Beyond, Johannes saw the tops of two British flags – the black and deep crimson Regimental Colour of the 58th Regiment and the brighter Union Flag of the Queen's Colour – as they came into view, moving lazily in the breathless air. For a second, he was struck by the intensity of the scene: the green of the grassy slope, the scarlet and dark-blue of the soldiers, and the distant shouts of their officers and men. Then, suddenly one of the men near him fired, prompting a ragged volley from his companions, and the scene was immediately obscured by a thick cloud of smoke thrown forward by their own rifles. Over the drum roll of the shots, Johannes could hear the shouts of the British drawing nearer, and a sudden breeze parted the smoke to show some of them just 50 yards away. But they were exposed to a continuous fire, their formation was on the verge of collapse and men were dropping in the grass. After a few minutes, the tone of the shouting changed, and Johannes caught a glimpse of the British falling back towards the crest. As they disappeared from view, a man on Johannes' right shouted something, stood up and ran forward; in the excitement of the

A Boer family 'on trek' in the 1870s. The Boer commando system reflected the essentially civilian needs of an agrarian society to protect itself rather than a professional military ethos.

moment Johannes scrambled after him. Running down the slope, he nearly stepped on something in the grass, and flinched as he realised it was a British soldier, lying with half his head blown away. Ahead of him, men had already reached the crest-line, and as he reached them Johannes looked down to see the British struggling down the steep slope below. Some had turned to fire back at the skyline, but the rest were in a ragged column stumbling down through the long grass and boulders. Here and there men were supporting their wounded comrades. In the centre, the great colours, torn and flapping now and

Boer hospitality: coffee, a pipe and exchanging news – pastimes as popular on commando as they were in everyday life.

ripped by bullets, fell and rose again as one bearer was shot, and another took up the burden. Suddenly there was a sharp concussion in the air nearby, the crack of a shell exploding, and a brittle spatter of shrapnel balls on the boulders. The British artillery had opened up to cover the retreat – and Johannes for one was glad to have the opportunity to hurry back to the protection of his trench.

The Battle of Laing's Nek was, in many ways, a defining moment in warfare in southern Africa. The history of the Boer farmers – the Afrikaans-speaking settlers from the Cape of Good Hope – had been characterised by conflict with the British imperial power, but Laing's Nek marked a distinct escalation in the level of violence, foreshadowing greater clashes to come. It was the first indication, too, that the battlefield tactics which had made the British the most powerful nation in the world might not be appropriate in an African context.[1] It demonstrated, too, the resolve of men such as Johannes de Bruyn, who never thought of himself as a soldier, but who belonged to a community whose determination to govern itself would lead Johannes into many more such conflicts over the coming decades.

In the 1870s, southern Africa was essentially divided between British colonies, Boer republics, and the last surviving vestiges of independent African kingdoms. The very existence of the Boer republics owed much to an antipathy towards the British. In 1652, Europeans had first established a permanent settlement on the extreme southern tip of the African continent when the Dutch East India Company built a small victualling (supply) station at the Cape of Good Hope. The Dutch had little interest in colonising Africa, but the outpost enabled them to service company ships on the long sea haul round Africa towards the far more profitable trading enclaves in the East Indies. A farming community was established to grow fresh fruit and vegetables for the sailors, and over the next century – and often in the face of official disapproval – these farmers began to expand into the hinterland, migrating into the good grazing lands which characterised the south-eastern seaboard. The original Dutch settlers were augmented by French immigrants – refugees from religious intolerance in Europe – and the community began to acquire a distinct frontier outlook of its

Members of the Pretoria Town commando in the field during the Mmalebogo campaign of 1894. All are armed with Martini-Henry rifles.

own. Tough, independent minded and conservative, and used to relying on their own resources, the settlers were suspicious of the company administration in faraway Cape Town. When, in 1806, the British – as part of the political twists and turns which characterised the global war against Napoleon – displaced the Dutch, the rift between metropolitan authority and frontier attitudes widened. Although British ambitions at the Cape were largely strategic, they found themselves inheritors of a growing conflict between the settlers on the Cape Frontier and a robust African society, the Xhosa. Over the next 30 years, British attempts to police the frontier led not only to sporadic violence, but to a growing alienation with the settlers. To the settlers, the British, with their international outlook and liberal views, seemed unsympathetic towards settler grievances and unable to offer protection against Xhosa attacks. By 1836, this disenchantment became so acute that hundreds of settler families simply opted to leave British territory, and establish new lands of their own in the interior.

This movement, a sporadic series of migrations lumped together under the name 'the Great Trek', shaped the political geography of southern Africa. It also gave a boost to the growing sense of cultural identity of the former Dutch settlers, who began to think of themselves as a distinct people known by a variety of names: Afrikanders, initially, then Afrikaners, meaning white Africans; or, more simply, burghers – citizen farmers – or Boers, countrymen. By the time the Trek had finished, Britain retained two colonies along the southern and eastern coastline – the Cape Colony and Natal – while the Boers administered two republics in the interior – the Orange Free State (*Oranje Vrystaat*) north of the Orange (Gairep) river, and the South African Republic (*Zuid-Afrikaanse Republiek*, popularly known as the Transvaal), across the Vaal (Sengqu) beyond.

Of course, the country occupied by the Boers had not been empty when they arrived, and the progress of the Trek was characterised by conflict with African groups. Boer settlement expanded rapidly across the sparsely populated arable land and Africans who challenged them were either driven away or reduced to the status of tenants on white farms. To the north and east, however, the Transvaal was surrounded by an arc of African groups – the Hanawa, Venda, Pedi and Transvaal Ndebele – who were entrenched in difficult terrain, and who never really acknowledged Boer authority until forced by military defeat to do so late in the century. In the Free State, the 1850s were marred by running conflicts with the most powerful local African group, the BaSotho of King Moshoeshoe.

Nor were the patterns of Boer settlement evenly spread. Since large tracts of land were often needed to support the Boer's herds, many farms were extremely large, and the towns – or dorps – which had sprung up to cater for their needs were small and widely separated. The same independence of spirit that had created the Trek movement led to constant fissures within Boer society, with many groups breaking away to establish tiny new republics on the periphery. These rose and fell, according to local fortunes, and were often absorbed back into the political body as a whole. Moreover, since there was a constant need for fresh grazing land, many Boers were tempted to intervene in the affairs of their African neighbours when circumstances permitted, often without official sanction. Thus Boer society had an expansionist dynamic which was out of all proportion to the numbers involved.

Members of the Pretoria Town commando at mess. Many men from this unit were *uitlanders*, and their appearance reflects their urban lifestyle.

The result was a continual underlying tension with African groups, set against a broader political rivalry with the British Empire. The British had relinquished their authority over the Trekkers only reluctantly, and in the 1870s had adopted a more aggressive and acquisitive policy in southern Africa. In 1877, on the pretext that the SAR (South African Republic) was unable to manage its affairs competently, Britain had annexed the Transvaal; four years later, in 1881, the Boers had overthrown British rule, but their victory merely paved the way for a far greater conflict which began in 1899 and only ended in 1902.

For many Boers, therefore, the late nineteenth century was a time of frequent conflicts, each of which severely tested the essentially agrarian and civilian nature of Boer society. For, until the very end of the period – and then only in limited numbers[2] – the Boers possessed no standing professional army on the European model, and Boer armies amounted to nothing more than a part-time civilian militia, lacking any sense of a professional military ethic, with no training in battlefield conditions and with an egalitarian spirit which was the antithesis of military discipline.

CHRONOLOGY

1876	SAR-Pedi War, north-eastern Transvaal.	1884	Unofficial intervention by SAR burghers in Zulu Civil War.
1879	Anglo-Zulu War (limited involvement of burghers from the Utrecht border district).	**5 June**	Battle of Tshaneni.
		1890	SAR expedition against the Lobedu of Queen Mujaji (northern Transvaal).
1879	Reduction of the Pedi kingdom by British Imperial forces.	1894	SAR expedition against the Hanawa of Chief Mmalebogo.
1881	Transvaal War of Independence (1st Boer War).		SAR expedition against the Tlou of Chief Makgoba (northern Transvaal).
28 January	Battle of Laing's Nek.	1895–96	Jameson Raid.
8 February	Battle of Schuinshoogte (Ingogo).	1898	SAR expedition against the Venda of Chief Mphefu (northern Transvaal).
27 February	Battle of Majuba.		
1881–84	Unofficial intervention by SAR burghers in Tswana conflicts.		
1882	SAR expedition against Chief Nyabela (Ndzundza Ndebele), eastern Transvaal.	1899–1902	Anglo-Boer War (*Tweede Vryheidsoorlog*; Second War of Freedom).

1899	**11 October**	Boer ultimatum expires; war begins.		**29 May**	Battles of Doornkop and Biddulphsberg.
	13 October	Boers besiege Mafeking.		**30 May**	British enter Johannesburg.
	15 October	Boers besiege Kimberley.		**5 June**	British enter Pretoria.
	20 October	Battle of Talana.		**7 June**	Battle of Roodewal.
	21 October	Battle of Elandslaagte.		**12 June**	Battle of Diamond Hill.
	24 October	Battle of Rietfontein.		**16 June**	British announce intention of burning farms of burghers still in the field.
	30 October	Battles of Pepworth and Nicholson's Nek; Boers besiege Ladysmith.		**31 July**	Surrender of Prinsloo in Brandwater Basin.
	23 November	Battle of Belmont.		**27 August**	Battle of Bergendal.
	25 November	Action at Graspan.		**19 October**	SAR President Paul Kruger leaves South Africa.
	28 November	Battle of Modder River.		**6–7 November**	Battle of Leliefontein.
	10 December	Battle of Stormberg.		**13 December**	Battle of Nooitgedacht.
	11 December	Battle of Magersfontein.		**16 December**	Boer Commandos under Kritzinger and Herzog invade Cape Colony.
	15 December	Battle of Colenso.	**1901**	**31 January**	Action at Modderfontein.
1900	**6 January**	Battle of Platrand (Wagon Hill).		**10 February**	De Wet invades the Cape Colony.
	23–24 January	Battle of Spion Kop.		**16 May**	Kritzinger attempts further invasion of the Cape.
	5–7 February	Battle of Vaalkrans.		**28 May**	Battle of Vlakfontein.
	14 February	British assault Thukela Heights.		**17 September**	Battles of Elandspoort and Blood River Poort.
	15 February	British relieve Kimberley.		**30 September**	Battle of Moedwil.
	18 February	Battle of Paardeberg.		**11 December**	Kritzinger's third attempt to invade the Cape.
	27 February	Surrender of Cronje at Paardeberg; British clear Thukela Heights.		**25 December**	Battle of Tweefontein.
	28 February	British relieve Ladysmith.	**1902**	**28 February**	Boer surrender at Lang Reit.
	7 March	Battle of Poplar Grove.		**7 March**	Battle of Tweebosch.
	10 March	Battle of Driefontein.		**11 April**	Battle of Roodewal.
	13 March	British occupy Bloemfontein.		**6 May**	Battle of Holkrans.
	15 March	British offer amnesty to Boers who surrender.		**15–31 May**	Peace negotiations at Vereeniging.
	31 March	Battle of Sannah's Post.			
	3–4 April	Battle of Mostertshoek.			
	5 April	Battle of Boshof.			
	12 May	Repulse of Boer attempt to capture Mafeking.			
	17 May	British relieve Mafeking.			

ENLISTMENT

In December 1880 Johannes de Bruyn, together with his father Hendrik and two of his brothers, had attended a meeting at a farm called Paardekraal to protest at the continued British occupation of the Transvaal. In a highly charged atmosphere, the meeting demanded that the British withdraw, and voted to use force to oppose them if necessary. A triumvirate (committee of three) of republican representatives was elected to serve as a provisional government. Within hours the first shots had been fired at British garrisons, and the triumvirate ordered its supporters to muster as commandos. Thus Johannes found himself for the first time caught up in events which would, temporarily at least, change him from a farmer's boy into a soldier.

The commando system lay at the heart of the Boer concept of military service. Essentially a temporary levy of armed farmers, gathered together to act as an armed unit, it had evolved on the Eastern Cape Frontier, where the scattered farms were often too widely separated to be protected by local garrisons, and where the farmers were at the mercy of African raiders. Traditionally, the men assembled at an appointed spot, each carrying their own weapons and provisions, and riding their own horses. While successive governments at the Cape recognised an obligation to provide ammunition and rations for an extended campaign, commandos were seldom in the field for long in the early days. They lacked the resources to feed themselves for any length of time, and in any case men were reluctant to be away from their farming duties and unprotected families for long. Once they had accomplished their objectives, they simply dispersed and went home.

At various times during the nineteenth century, attempts were made to enforce the provisions of commando service by law, but many aspects of the system were never codified, although they were generally understood and accepted by the men they affected. It was not until 1898 that the SAR passed specific commando laws which effectively made service compulsory.

A commando assembles in a small rural town – a scene which would have preceded most of the military action in the two republics across the period.

All men between the ages of 16 and 60 were expected to attend commando muster. Johannes was not unusual in that, in 1881, he fought alongside his father and brothers; it was common for all the men from one family to serve together. Indeed, it was not unknown for men considerably over the age of 60 to fight, and boys as young as 11 or 12 took to the field under the pretext of performing chores for their elder brothers or fathers. Black Africans living in the republics were not subject to commando service, although many accompanied their employers in the role of servants. White settlers who were not Afrikaners by descent were, however, liable to serve, a fact thrown into sharp relief on the eve of the Anglo-Boer War of 1899–1902. In 1885 gold had been discovered in unprecedented quantities in the Transvaal, and foreign miners flooded in to exploit it, having a profound effect on the demographic make-up of the white population. Fearing that they would lose power to these *uitlanders* – foreigners – the Republic refused to allow them voting rights. The *uitlanders* were, nonetheless, still required to give commando service, and their complaints about the injustice of their position were seized upon by the British to justify intervention in the Republic's affairs.

The republics were divided into electoral districts, each administered by a *landdrost* or magistrate, which were then further sub-divided into wards headed by a *veldt-kornet* (field cornet). Each district was required to provide a commando when called upon. The commandos varied in size according to the level of the white farming population, and attendance was nominally compulsory, with fines or confiscation of property being the penalty for refusal. However, since perhaps the most overriding characteristic of Boer society was an unwillingness to submit without question to any form of authority, evasion of commando service was not

The commando from the town of Ladybrand in the Orange Free State assemble on the eve of war in 1899. The smart city clothes and light hats are typical of the appearance of commandos from the urban areas at the beginning of the war.

Four sons of Petrus Lefras Uys, photographed in the 1870s. Their appearance is typical of burghers at this period – three carry 'Monkey Tail' carbines and the fourth a Westley-Richards 'falling-block' carbine.
(Killie Campbell Collection)

uncommon, and often carried little social stigma. Wealthy or influential individuals sometimes appointed proxies to stand in their place, while the common acceptance of the priorities of agricultural life meant that many men were able to plead that they were simply too busy on their farms to serve. Most Boers were passionately committed to the idea that they were free burghers, not soldiers, and that they were bound by a feeling of common service towards the community, and not by any form of military authority or discipline.

All officials within the commandos were elected – the commanding officer, or commandant, *veldt-kornets* and corporals – and their leadership depended largely on the willingness of their men to follow them. Even in battle, it was not unusual for individual burghers to simply refuse to obey commands which they did not like, while consistently unpopular officers faced being voted down. All decisions, from grand strategy down to daily duties, were subject to approval by a *krygsraad*, a council of war in which the most ordinary burgher was as entitled to his say as the commanding officer.

As a result of this, many commandos, certainly until the end of 1899, often had a parochial outlook that reflected the priorities and hierarchy of their local communities. At the beginning of a campaign, officers were often elected according to their standing within the community, or as a result of extended family patronage. In 1879, for example, when Britain went to war with the Zulu kingdom, an attempt was made to recruit Boers from the newly annexed Transvaal to fight against what the British hoped the Boers would perceive as a common enemy. In fact, Boer society at the time was so opposed to the annexation that most refused to join the British; the one exception was a commando led by Petrus Lefras Uys, a prominent farmer in the Utrecht district, an area of 'disputed territory' where Zulu and Boer territorial claims overlapped. Uys' security depended on the reduction of Zulu power, and many of the men who took to the field with him were his neighbours, tied to him by family links, friendship or a common vulnerability.

Uys proved an able field commander until his death in action at the Battle of Hlobane (28 March 1879), but men elected on the strength of peacetime influence did not always make the best commanders. Their shortcomings often emerged in protracted campaigning, whether they were too old for the rigours of life in the field, too cautious, too rash, or simply incompetent. In such circumstances they were often replaced by men of proven ability, and this was particularly the case after March 1900 when, following the collapse of the Boer armies during the conventional phase of the Anglo-Boer War, many senior commandants retired from the field, to be replaced by more dynamic natural leaders such as de la Rey, de Wet, Botha and Smuts.

The commando system reflected the predominantly individualistic and local outlook of most Boer communities – a loyalty to relatives, friends and neighbours and a commitment to certain common ideals rather than a broader loyalty to the state. Support for campaigns waged a long way from home was liable to suffer if the risks and hardships outweighed the immediate sense of danger. Many burghers were simply unwilling to leave their own farms to travel long distances and fight in a cause which had little relevance to themselves. This was undoubtedly a factor in the disastrous Transvaal war against the Pedi king Sekhukhune in 1876, when burghers from commandos in the central districts showed a marked reluctance to leave their farms at a busy time of the year to fight on the north-eastern borders, and morale throughout the campaign suffered as a result. When a *krygsraad* condemned burghers who had refused to storm a defended Pedi position, the commando responded with a petition that stated bluntly, 'We are all entirely unwilling to storm Seceoconi's Mountain for the reason that we see no chance of safeguarding our lives or conquering the [Pedi].'

On the other hand, if a threat was considered sufficiently serious, it often provided the most effective catalyst in motivating the Boer community as a whole to fight. This was certainly the case in 1880-81, and to an even greater extent in 1899, when British authority was considered to be so hostile to the entire Boer way of life that Boer society was largely united by the need to oppose it. In a broad sense, Johannes de Bruyn and many like him were motivated to fight in 1881 and again in 1899 by patriotism – by a fervent attachment to the concept of the Boer lifestyle, and by a fierce sense of the freedom which it inspired. On those occasions Johannes was not influenced by the prospect of pay – if offered to the commandos at all, it was certainly erratic – or by any sense of military glory, which was utterly alien to him. The concept of honour on the battlefield, so carefully inculcated among professional European armies as a means of enhancing discipline and resolve, was entirely irrelevant to men who simply looked upon war as a means of resolving an immediate difficulty in order that they might return to their ordinary lives. As one Boer memorably put it, 'You English fight to die; we fight to live.'

Yet on occasions the Boers could be tempted to fight by the prospect of profit, not so much in coin or material possessions, but in cattle and land. The underlying expansionism of Boer society created a constant need for new arable land and cattle, particularly among large farming families with many sons. In that regard, Boer society was often in direct competition with African societies who defined wealth and prestige in

Commandant Uys and his sons a few years later – in the field during the Anglo-Zulu War. One of Uys' sons still carries a Westley-Richards, with cartridges held in the pockets in his waistcoat – the rest have Martini-Henry rifles, probably supplied by the British. Note Uys' sun-helmet and conspicuous hunting knife. Uys himself was killed at the Battle of Hlobane on 28 March 1879.

the same terms. Despite the fact that many African societies had armed themselves with firearms, they were usually obsolete models in poor condition, and were easily outclassed by Boer groups equipped with modern weapons. Throughout the 1880s and 1890s, the Boers offered a decisive battlefield element among African societies collapsing into internal conflict as a result of European political and economic penetration.

In 1883, Johannes himself was tempted to take part in one such expedition. In 1879, the British had broken up the Zulu kingdom, and in an attempt to destroy the influence of the Zulu Royal House had imposed a divisive post-war settlement. Within a few years Zululand had split into pro- and anti-royalist factions. In 1883, the restored King Cetewayo was heavily defeated by anti-royalists led by *inkhosi* Zibhebhu ka Maphitha. When Cetewayo died the following year, the royalist cause seemed on the verge of ruin. His heir, Prince Dinuzulu, appealed to the Boers of the SAR to support him. Although the government refused to be dragged into purely Zulu affairs, some 350 Boers formed a volunteer commando and offered their services to Dinuzulu. George Mossop, an English-speaking settler who had grown up among Boer hunters in the Transvaal, and had fought in the Anglo-Zulu War, described how he and his companions came to volunteer:

> Dinizulu, the son of Cetewayo, is getting the worst of it, and he has asked for assistance. If we assist him, and he conquers Usibebu, he will give us the northern part of Zululand, which will be cut up into farms, and we will each get one if we go and help.' ... It appeared to me a wild undertaking, filibustering into Zululand on the off-chance of getting a grant of land from a Zulu chief ... [but] the idea appealed to me. I reckoned I would have a shot at it. It would not cost much ... 'I will go', I said, 'when will we make a start?' 'Ja nee,' [my friend] replied, 'a farm is a farm, and unless we get there quickly we will be too late to get one.'

On 5 June 1884 a combined royalist and Boer force decisively defeated Zibhebhu at the Battle of Tshaneni, an action which demonstrated the effectiveness of the Boers' awesome firepower. As a result, Prince Dinuzulu allowed the volunteers to claim farms in Zululand. Although this move antagonised the British in neighbouring Natal, who forced the Boers to limit their claims, a significant area – around Hlobane mountain and the Transvaal border – was taken by the Boers. Johannes himself received a large farm for his part in the expedition; the Boers declared themselves to be a New Republic (*Nieue Republiek*) and built as a capital

In 1899, the SAR exploited the railway network to move supplies and reinforcements to the main battle fronts.

the town of Vryheid ('Freedom'). Similar ambitions prompted Boer intervention among the unsettled Tswana groups on the western Transvaal borders around the same time.

TRAINING

Johannes' grandfather, *Oom* Koos, had settled his farm near Heidelburg during the Great Trek. At that time, the rolling grasslands of the high veldt were still teeming with game, and *Oom* Koos had lived entirely by his own resources, building his farm and surviving in an environment not then affected by efficient European hunting methods. Even by Johannes' time, this was beginning to change, and he was perhaps one of the last generation who, as young men, witnessed the wildlife of the interior in something like its original state. By the 1870s, teams of professional hunters, exploiting the herds for their hides, horns and meat, had wrought carnage among the animals, and by 1880 the herds had disappeared in all but the most remote parts of the country. For young Boers who grew to manhood in the last 20 years of the decade, the old hunting and Voortrekker lives (the pioneers of the 1830s – literally 'those who trek to the fore') were already a thing of myth.

Nonetheless, Johannes himself still grew up accustomed to life in the open air. At the age of 11 his father taught him how to shoot, and from that point he took his share of the work on remote parts of the farm, learning to ride a horse in rugged and stony terrain, to stay in the saddle when the horse shied at snakes or side-stepped to avoid the holes dug by ant-bears (*aardvarks*). He learned to endure the extremes of the high-veldt weather, the baking heat of summer days and the sudden storms of the evenings, with their torrential downpours, and the crisp frosty nights of winter. He learned, too, how to survive for days at a time on hard-baked rusks – a traditional farm staple – and sun-dried meat, known as biltong, washed down in the evening with coffee cooked over a campfire.

His shooting was of an entirely practical nature. No professional hunter himself, he lacked their limitless experience, but he learned to judge distance in the clear air which characterised the interior, to anticipate the twists and turns of a moving target, and to kill cleanly and efficiently. Schooled in shooting for the pot, he was concerned not to waste cartridges which could be expensive and difficult to replace.

Like most Boers raised on a farm, Johannes depended upon his horse. The horses favoured by the Boers were a type known generally as the 'BaSotho Pony'. Traded or stolen from the Dutch by the Sotho of the southern Kahlamba mountains early in the nineteenth century, these had been shaped by natural selection to form a distinct breed. They were small and hardy, used to life among the rocky and hilly terrain,

The enduring image of burghers on commando *c.*1900 – mounted, carrying Mausers, and slung round with ammunition bandoliers.

with remarkable stamina and endurance. Accustomed to foraging for themselves, they had adapted to Africa's wide range of grasses, and periods of drought had bred in them a capacity to survive without water for longer than their European forebears. Like his father, Johannes rode with his legs thrust out straight in the stirrups, and even on long rides burdened his horse with a minimum of equipment – no more than his saddlebags and a blanket tied to the back of the saddle.

If need be, Johannes could fire his rifle from the saddle with a good chance of scoring a hit. Generally, however, he preferred to dismount, stalking his target on foot, skirmishing from cover to cover so as not to be spotted. This technique, learned in hunting wildlife, would prove equally effective against human targets.

It was this self-reliant farm life that served Johannes as the basis for his military training. He could ride, shoot and survive in the bush by his own resources; he had a good eye for the country, he could think for himself and act on his own initiative. On the other hand, he had no concept of the ethics of military discipline, and only the vaguest idea of the teamwork necessary to function as part of an effective battlefield unit. Something of the latter he learned by experience; the former he never considered a trait worth learning.

Johannes fought in the two great wars against the British, in 1880-81 and again in 1899–1902. During the first war, he found his colleagues to be very much like himself: farmers from the countryside, often serving with members of their families. In 1899, however, when he fought with the Vryheid commando, Johannes noticed the effects of 20 years of change among Afrikaner society. True, a significant majority of the commandos were still country dwellers, but the influx into the Transvaal following the discovery of gold had led to a growth in urban development. Many of the old magisterial districts now mustered two commandos – one raised in the rural areas, and another from the urban population. Moreover, the cattle disease rinderpest, which had swept through southern Africa in the 1890s, had ruined some parts of the farming community completely, and these 'poor whites' had drifted to the towns. When the Vryheid commando joined the general muster on the borders of British Natal in October 1899, Johannes was surprised to see that many Boers from the urban areas lacked horses or wagons, had little experience of life on the veldt and had never hunted for the pot.

Nevertheless, they still retained many of the elements of Boer society which would make them better suited to the coming conflict than their British counterparts – a tradition of self-reliance and a passionate commitment to the survival of their way of life.

Life in the field; a group of burghers in camp at Colesberg, February 1900. Note the typical shelter, a mixture of tents and tarpaulins, and the strips of biltong hanging out to dry. Even at this time, these men are armed with British Lee-Metfords.

DAILY LIFE

When Johannes and his family went to war they took with them an ox-wagon from the farm, loaded with camping equipment and supplies, and several African servants to help with the chores of life in the veldt.

Life on trek

The ox-wagon had become a symbol of Boer mobility, independence and self-reliance during the Great Trek period, and it was still regarded as an essential accompaniment to life on campaign until the end of the century. It served as both a means of transport, a mobile camping ground, and a method of defence. Although the Transvaal government made an attempt to supply the commandos with tents on campaign – particularly in 1899 – many Boers preferred to live out of their wagons, stretching a tarpaulin from the side of the wagon and supporting it on poles to provide an effective and airy shelter. If the wagon was tented – covered in canvas attached to hoops above the wagon-bed – or half-tented, this in itself would serve as overnight accommodation. At worst, men could always sleep on the ground itself under the wagon-bed.

It was common for Boers on campaign to camp in defensive wagon laagers. In their simplest form, these were wagon circles, formed by running the pole (or *disselboom*) of each wagon under the one in front. Laagers could be secured by lashing the wagons together with heavy leather straps and filling the gaps between them with thorn bushes. As such, they were largely invulnerable to attacks by an enemy lacking firearms and equipped only with close-quarter weapons – as the African enemies of the 1830s usually were.

The laager tradition had by no means died out by the last quarter of the nineteenth century. In both 1881 and 1899, laagers were used as camps behind the front lines. Nor was this entirely anachronistic, as the wars against the African groups in the 1890s demonstrated that laagers still provided an effective means of defence, particularly against surprise night-attacks. Nevertheless, the vulnerability of the laager system against an enemy armed with effective modern weapons was brutally demonstrated in the battles on the Modder River front in early 1900. The wagons were found to offer little protection against shell or even small-arms fire, and the people and animals contained within were effectively trapped. Moreover, they hampered Boer mobility to such an extent that it was impossible to break up the laagers and escape before being cut off by British cavalry. In the end, the Boers trapped at Paardeberg had little option but to surrender. Although the Boers would never entirely abandon their attachment to ox-wagons, those commandos who were most effective during the guerrilla phase of the war tended to be those with the most streamlined transport element.

Feeding the commandos

Providing food for the assembled commandos was always problematic. Because the Boers were not a regular army, no official commissariat existed to supply them in the field. Traditionally, the men who fought with the early commandos brought with them their own supplies, and even in 1899 there remained a commitment to provide food for the first few days of an expedition. For the most part, the various campaigns

The problem of supply was a perennial theme of commando life; here supplies are requisitioned from sympathetic townsfolk.

between 1876 and 1902 were not, however, short affairs and it was clearly impractical to expect large concentrations of men to provision themselves for months on end. The government of the SAR accepted a responsibility to supply its commandos with food, but the supply was usually erratic.

In 1881 the short duration of the war and the limited numbers involved mitigated against serious hardship. Furthermore, many Boers were able to supply themselves privately from stores nearby.

The experience for the storekeepers – many of whom were close to the border and sympathetic to the British cause – was, according to a British correspondent, Thomas Carter, who covered the 1881 campaign, mixed:

At Franklyn's store the Boers had behaved very well, paying for everything, and comporting themselves with decorum. Here provisions were not scarce, except breadstuffs and alcoholic beverages, which had long since been consumed … I learnt from Mr Johnson, who has a farm on the border, that the Boers had not done much damage to his house. They had helped themselves to necessaries, including wood-work fit for making coffins. Some of his sheep and horses were missing, the latter having been in the hands of the Boers. At an adjoining farm, that of Mr. Tom Minter, a very different state of things was revealed to the owner when he visited the place. Here the damage had been wilful …

Unfortunately he had incurred the displeasure of the Boers, and this was the nature of their revenge. At Walker's the Boers had all along behaved very well. He has a store and canteen combined, and whatever the Boers wanted they paid for, and behaved civilly to the proprietor and his family from first to last.

Nevertheless such pragmatic means of resupply, the same observer noted that the Boers seemed to be suffering shortages in other regards, for he met several individuals whose:

Clothing was ragged, their accoutrements patched and shabby; their rifles were the only clean things about them, and comprised their sole weapons … some [were] on foot, without boots or stockings, some mounted, but all armed.

The situation had not greatly improved by the time of the SAR's expedition against the Hanawa of Chief Mmalebogo in 1894. The Rev. Colin Rae, who accompanied the expedition, remarked scathingly that:

It was difficult to understand how, with a force of such dimensions, the most important department (the commissariat) had been so grossly neglected; but such had proved the case, for the total supplies loaded up in Pretoria consisted … of four packets of sugar, fifteen bags of meal, a few boxes of candles, and one bag of rice (the latter almost unfit for food), and this was supposed to be sufficient for the requirements of six hundred men. Had it not been for the fact that most of the messes had privately provided themselves with extra provisions, over and above the eight days' rations expected of them, starvation pure and simple would have had to be faced when only half the journey had been accomplished. As to blankets and clothing, the amount issued was not worth mentioning.

In the early stages of the conventional war, supplies were shipped to the front by train, and collected by representatives from the commandos who took them out to the laagers. Here wagons loaded with supplies arrive in a camp outside Ladysmith.

If anything, the supply of food, spare clothing and tents was worse on the outbreak of war in 1899. Despite the fact that the SAR had been preparing for war, the huge numbers of men mobilised – some 40,000 – stretched the commissariat to breaking point[3]. Slaughter animals were supplied to the army assembled on the Natal border from government reserves, and the Boers invaded the British colony accompanied by large herds of cattle and sheep, giving it to Johannes' mind the appearance of a Biblical exodus. The government undertook to supply bread, flour, coffee, sugar and salt, and in theory these were either bought from civilian contractors or requisitioned from the businesses of *uitlanders* who had fled on the outbreak of war. Large supplies of spare clothes were also bought up by the government, usually according to availability rather than suitability. Stocks of urban clothes in warehouses in Johannesburg and Pretoria were sent to the front, and on occasion consisted of lightweight cotton clothes and straw hats which did not long survive the rigours of life in the veldt. Sewing circles organised among patriotic Afrikaner women produced better results, but the distribution of all supplies was chaotic. For the most part, supplies were sent to the front by train, and then loaded onto wagons at the railhead to go forward to the laagers. It was not unusual for sacks of flour to be left on the platform and be exposed to the elements for days at a time – and to be quite inedible by the time they reached the commandos. Moreover, the system was ripe for abuse, with men helping themselves to their own requirements at each stage in the journey, and those actually serving in the front-line trenches receiving little more than the left-overs. When the Boer lines began to collapse on all fronts in early 1900, and the British pushed their advance into the heart of the republics, the government supply system broke down entirely.

As a result, across the period, life in the commandos was seldom pleasant. It meant camping out in all weathers, living in shoes that fell apart after weeks of scrambling over rocks and boulders, and in clothes which were snagged and torn on thorn bushes and aloes. It was fortunate that those from a farming background were prepared to

A camp outside Ladysmith – a tarpaulin has been erected over a wagon to provide a shelter.

assume the burden of their own provisioning, because there soon became little else, and, as in most armies, finding food became a daily preoccupation. Between 1876 and 1900, most burghers in commandos subsisted on beef from slaughter animals, roasted on campfires or boiled in pots, or cut into strips and dried in the sun as biltong. Flour, when it was available, was baked into bread, or made into dumplings and fried in fat. Most men fell back on traditional farmer's fare such as rusks, which were baked by their womenfolk and somehow sent to the front, even during the last stages of the guerrilla war in 1901-02. Vegetables were a luxury, and often only obtained by foraging.

In the 1870s and 1880s, many Boers were used to shooting for the pot, and subsidised their rations on campaign by hunting. In the 1890s game was less plentiful, and in 1899 the SAR banned burghers from shooting animals out of a concern for ammunition wastage and the corrosive effects on discipline of unauthorised hunting expeditions. However, as the war went on, and commandos operated increasingly without reference to government authority, some hunting did occur out of sheer necessity.

One great luxury of life in the veldt was coffee. An essential part of daily routine on the farm, and the focus of much peacetime social interaction, the brewing and drinking of coffee was the subject of much informal ritual; like many of his colleagues Johannes de Bruyn felt he could endure almost all the hardships of active service providing he had access to a handful of coffee beans, water and at least a tin mug. One foreign volunteer serving with the Boers during the 1899–1902 campaign heard them comment frequently that 'without coffee we can't make war'. Sugar, readily available in peacetime, was often one of the first items to become scarce, and was prized accordingly.

Those burghers who had access to a wagon took what comforts they could with them on campaign. Small wooden stools were popular as an alternative to sitting on rocks or squatting on the ground, while most Boers started out a campaign with a three-legged iron cooking pot, a coffee pot, tin or enamel mugs and plates, and some sort of cutlery. As expeditions wore on, however, these items were often lost, and men were forced to improvise replacements.

Commando duties

By definition, the everyday life of a burgher on commando was essentially one of active service. Nonetheless, when not actively fighting, there was little enough routine to his day. Sentry duty was one military habit which was indispensable and each corporalship selected sentries for day and night duty, and rotated them amongst themselves. George

Mossop, serving with Lukas Meyer's commando in Zululand in 1884, was appointed sentry one evening, and was still unrelieved the next morning. When he went to complain to his corporal the corporal's reply neatly summed up the dilemma faced by those in authority within the commandos. 'Man,' he said, 'I did my best. I pleaded to every man in the laager, but no one would budge, and I was at length obliged to go to bed myself.' There was little professional formality about the job, and the sentries merely took up a position ocommanding feature and made themselves as comfortable as possible. Mounted patrols were sent out beyond the sentry outposts to watch for enemy movements. In baking sun or pouring rain, such duty could be unpleasant, and it was common to improvise shelters from blankets or tarpaulins. Some more diligent commandants attempted to impose watchwords on their sentries, but the idea was essentially alien, and often caused confusion. When not on sentry duty, the Boers filled their time with the ordinary pursuits of camp life – slaughtering animals and burying the offal for sanitary reasons, preparing food, collecting water and firewood, and tending to the horses.

'Boers on Outpost, 1899-00' – a pair of typically lightly equipped burghers early in the war.

To help him in these tasks, Johannes and many of his colleagues took African servants with them on commando. These men were family retainers from their home farms, and were generally known as *agterryers* ('after-riders' or grooms), although their duties went much further than simply feeding and caring for the horses. They performed a great deal of manual labour around the camps, and were in great demand to prepare front-line trenches, an uncomfortable job in the sweltering sun which was unpopular with the burghers themselves. Johannes de Bruyn's *agterryer* served him first as a young man in 1881, and continued to accompany him into the field in later expeditions. This was despite the fact that, like many African servants on Boer farms, his family had been largely dispossessed when *Oom* Koos had claimed his farm in the 1830s, and only those who were required to work as labourers were allowed to remain on their traditional lands. Nevertheless, many *agterryers* took an active part in successive campaigns, and, despite the fact that the Boers, who knew the terrain very well, tended to employ armed African scouts much less than the British, some even fought in the front line. Most remained in service until the general collapse of the conventional war in 1900, when the majority of non-combatant personnel returned home. Although their contribution to the campaigns across this period is often overlooked, it was essential to the Boer war effort.

Because of the essentially egalitarian nature of the commando system, discipline was far more relaxed among the Boers than in professional armies. The burghers were not bound by military law, and such regulations as there were tended to reflect a sense of common good. Government prohibitions were few, and it was left to most commandos to decide their own regulations by *krygsraad*. Although most commandants officially frowned on absence without leave, the punishments were usually mild and only enforced in extreme cases, since it was widely recognised that men might have pressing farming or family commitments at home which required their attention. Even during periods of prolonged action, it was common for men simply to go home to sort out their affairs. Stealing from comrades and sleeping on sentry duty were punishable offences, although many burghers complained that in the confusion of camp life useful pieces of equipment nonetheless often found new and unauthorised owners. Corporal punishment, while not unknown, was rare, since many burghers were uncomfortable at the degree of public humiliation it entailed. If burghers were flogged, the punishment was usually confined to a few strokes with a stirrup leather – although some commandants dispensed summary justice in the heat of the moment with a hide whip known as a *sjambok*. Punishment for Africans who deserted their employers in the field or, worse, were thought to be in league with the enemy, was often much more severe, and serious floggings or even execution were not unknown. More typically, punishments for burghers consisted of extra duties, fines, or the rough-and-ready humiliation of being tossed in an ox-hide. This was a well-known piece of farmers' horseplay, in which slits were cut in the edges of an ox-hide to serve as handles, and the miscreant was tossed on the hide by a group of his colleagues. Scrapes, bruises and the laughter of the onlookers were the result.

Indeed, a lack of excessive respect towards authority was a marked characteristic of Boer commando life. Commandants could be, and often were, required to justify their decisions not only to the *krygsraad* but to the most ordinary man on commando. This applied not only to matters of strategy or tactics, but to the everyday management of the campaign. Burghers were entitled to question the commandant on matters as varied as the immediate military objectives, the unfairness of horse-guarding rotas or the whereabouts of missing personal possessions.

Pastimes on commando
The nature of Boer warfare meant that – certainly in the last quarter of the nineteenth century – there was often a good deal of time spent in idleness as the commandos waited to starve out an African enemy, or held defensive positions in anticipation of a British attack. To fill this time the burghers relied on their own ingenuity. Organised events offering popular farmers' sports – known as *boeresport* – were popular, and included events such as football, races, sack- and three-legged races, and the long jump. Young burghers – known to their elders as *penkoppe*, an allusion to young and frisky male animals, whose horns are just beginning to develop – often livened up life in the laagers by playing practical jokes. Johannes himself, during his first campaign in 1881, had found and killed a puff adder near the camp, and had delighted in hiding the dead snake under a wagon where a friend was accustomed to sleep. Pelting unsuspecting colleagues with wild fruit or placing blank cartridges in fires to explode were other popular pranks. Many burghers simply took the opportunities afforded by quiet periods to snooze in the

shade, or to swap stories with the members of their corporalship. A burgher named P.S. Lombard, on the Mafeking front, recalled that one day early in the war he smoked his pipe until his mouth was sore, drank coffee until fit to burst, and told every story he knew – and was then disappointed to find it was still only midday! In the evening, around the campfire, men sipped coffee and perhaps played the harmonica, or, if they had one, the concertina. Many rural Boers were illiterate, but on prolonged campaigns news from home was always prized, and men who could do so read out letters to their illiterate colleagues, and took down the replies. For educated or urbanised Boers, books, newspapers and magazines were a luxury, and were sought after with delight in overrun British camps. Many more conservative burghers believed that such works were frivolous, however, and that the only appropriate reading matter was the Holy Bible. Roland Schikkerling, an educated Boer in the Johannesburg commando, noted that most burghers carried a pocket Bible with them on campaign, and that during quiet periods it was common to see them passing an afternoon seeking solace in the scriptures in the shade.

Drink and tobacco

Smoking was a great luxury. An inevitable accompaniment to social interaction between men on the farm, it remained so on commando duty. Johannes had considered himself very much a man in 1881, smoking coarse tobacco from a clay pipe around the campfire, and listening to his elders discussing the war. In 1881 and again during the African campaigns of the 1890s, the burghers were largely responsible for their own supplies of tobacco, but in 1899 the SAR made an attempt to supply its men in this regard. The supply was, of course, erratic, and as the war progressed tobacco became a highly prized commodity. During the guerrilla phase, many men were reduced to eking out their supplies with dried pumpkin, potato or peach leaves, and indeed burghers who claimed knowledge of the properties of particular wild leaves as a tobacco substitute became increasingly popular among their colleagues.

While some commandos in 1899 enjoyed a reputation for hard drinking – particularly those from towns such as Johannesburg, where canteens and pubs were very much a feature of civilian life – most Boers were temperate in their drinking habits. Some had religious objections to alcohol; others only drank at home on special occasions, and found the scarcity of alcohol in the field did not alter this situation. Indeed, in

1899 the SAR banned the sale of alcohol to commandos, although there was no ban on individual burghers procuring their own. However, supplies brought from home soon diminished, and the only hope of resupply was by family gifts, from civilian stores, or by looting from British camps. In 1881 Johannes had enjoyed his first taste of gin – known as 'square face' at the time, from the shape of the bottle – in the laagers below Majuba hill, but by 1899 his taste had matured to brandy, and he took with him a flask to keep out the cold on sentry duty. Some burghers, particularly those from commandos based in the northern Transvaal, had a preference for a strong fruit brandy, known as *mampoer*, which was distilled in those parts.

APPEARANCE, DRESS AND WEAPONS

Throughout the nineteenth century, the Boers took to the field in their everyday civilian clothes. Although many possessed smart clothes for Church services or special occasions, these were hardly appropriate for life in the veldt in all weathers, and instead they mustered for commando service in their most hard-wearing farming clothes. As such, they presented a generally drab appearance which led many professional soldiers – including their British enemy – to consistently underestimate their fighting qualities. In 1881, one British officer could scarcely conceal his contempt when describing the average Boer:

> A dirty, unkempt fellow, with long hair and beard, very much tanned, his face the colour of mahogany, a generally broad-shouldered, hard-looking man, his dress of all sorts of conditions – usually a coat that will just hold together, and a pair of baggy corduroy trousers. The chances are he had one spur on upside down, his head covered with a broad-brimmed felt hat, high in crown, and a dirty flannel shirt.

A generation later, towards the end of the 1899–1902 war, another British officer admitted that:

> What is more humiliating than anything else, is the realization that these miserable creatures are an enemy able to keep the flower of England's army in check … and render abortive a military reputation built upon unparalleled traditions.

However their appearance struck outsiders, there were some changes in civilian fashion from 1876 to 1902 which affected the appearance of Boer troops in the field. In 1881, Johannes had fought in a

Burghers captured during the fighting at Zwartkopjes, outside Pretoria, in 1881. They have been disarmed, but their appearance is typical of the men who fought in the Transvaal revolt.

loose-fitting double-breasted jacket and trousers of heavy corduroy. Often described in contemporary accounts as yellow in colour, this in fact soon became weathered to a myriad of shades from light buff to tobacco brown. Such clothes were popular in the farming community at the time, and were issued in large quantities by British troops to their irregular and auxiliary units. Nevertheless, since personal choice was the guiding factor, many of Johannes' colleagues in that war wore jackets and trousers of coarse cloth in various shades of brown on grey. Contemporary photographs suggest that the wide-brimmed hats – essential as a protection against sun and rain – of the 1870s and 1880s still reflected the fashion for broad brims which had been popular among the Voortrekkers.

A typical Boer commando in the Free State c. 1880. Note the sun-helmet worn by the commandant.

By the 1890s, the old yellow corduroy had largely disappeared, and with the growth in the white population of the republics a greater range of clothing had become commercially available. In 1899, most rural burghers wore single-breasted jackets and hats with less extravagant brims.

Waistcoats were popular across the period, not only as a means of keeping warm on cool days, but also for storing ammunition. In the 1870s and 1880s, the age of single-shot, breach-loading firearms, waistcoat pockets were a handy means of storing cartridges. These could either be slipped into ordinary pockets, or carried in loops stitched into the waistcoat for the purpose. Thomas Carter left a vivid description of the appearance of Boers gathering up British weapons in the aftermath of Majuba:

> His waistcoat had strips of leather sewn all over it from the bottom button to the throat; these clips were filled with cartridges; the man was a moving armoury in himself … he was an old fellow, fully fifty-five years of age, short and stout, with shaggy beard, whiskers, and eyebrows … There were lads there not more than fifteen, and old men of fifty or more, all armed to the teeth; every one with more rifles, bayonets and ammunition than he could possibly carry.

By the 1890s, the waistcoats had altered in design to enable them to carry clips of rounds, and some were produced in a webbing material.

During the Voortrekker period, the most popular type of footwear were home-made hide shoes, known as *velskoen*. Tanned, supple and comfortable to wear, they required a degree of experience and skill to produce, but once learned the art could be easily turned to good effect whenever an old pair of shoes wore out. Johannes de Bruyn, fighting his

The Free State General W. Kolbe c.1900. There is nothing about his appearance to indicate his rank; he wears a rosette in OFS colours on his lapel.

first campaign in 1881, rode out from his father's farm wearing *velskoen*, and indeed many burghers continued to wear them across the period, despite the increasing availability of shop-bought, leather lace-up shoes and boots. In the 1870s, some men preferred to wear leather gaiters, laced at the side which were popular among mounted irregular units fighting for the British for their practicality in protecting the lower legs. These had largely disappeared by the 1890s, and while a few affluent burghers wore leather riding boots, ordinary shoes were by far the norm at the outbreak of war in 1899.

It was unusual for commandants to appear in anything different from their men. A few favoured the long black tailcoats which were worn by men of authority at Church gatherings, but these seldom survived long in the field. During the 1870s, some commandants affected the habit of wearing sun helmets, which were worn by British officials at the time. Others preferred ordinary hats with a taller crown – demi-tophats – to make them stand out. By 1899, however, even these distinctions had largely died out, and it was only the presence of expensive personal items such as revolvers (worn on straps over the shoulder, rather than around the waist) and field glasses, which served as a distinction of rank. Ironically, however, as the war passed into the guerrilla phase, and many commandants ran increasingly streamlined commando units, some commandants – Botha included – opted to wear light khaki suits which had a distinctly uniform look about them.

In the wars of the 1890s, Boers from the urban settlements often looked distinctly different from their rural counterparts. The distinction could be detected not only in their dress, but in their manner. Many turned out for commando duty in clothes which reflected town fashions – light cotton jackets, smart waistcoats, straw hats or even bowlers. The Rev. Colin Rae saw the Pretoria commando mustering for the Mmalebogo expedition in 1894:

> Some of the men had little idea of what was required, as evidenced by their general get up, a loud check suit, straw hat, and tennis shoes, with cartridge belt put on upside down, scarcely betokened a smart military appearance. One fellow had his gun-strap so mixed up with that of his canteen that it would have taken him some time to 'present arms'. Others took no rations with them whatever, but laughingly remarked that they did not intend to starve nonetheless. The Boers were all mounted; many of the Pretoria Town contingent, however (mostly Englishmen), had no horses, and preferred keeping to the wagons rather than doing stable duty.

The lack of preparedness implicit in this description was exposed by the Jameson Raid in 1895-96, when many burghers answered the call without even weapons to fight. To some extent this situation had been rectified by 1899 – and certainly most *uitlanders* had left the Transvaal rather than fight against the British – but the differences in appearance, manner and experience between the rural and urban commandos, noted by Rae, still lingered, and occasionally emerged in bickering in the field. Rural commandos sometimes complained that their urban counterparts assumed social airs, and received better provisions than those from the countryside.

Throughout the period, very little attempt was made to add an element of uniformity to Boer costume. Coloured puggarees – lengths of cloth wound around the hat – and ribbons were sometimes worn to suggest allegiance to a particular commando. Free State burghers sometimes wore orange hatbands, and Transvaalers green; at various times in the 1899–1902 war some commandos distinguished themselves with white or yellow bands. Commandant Danie Theron's famous unit of scouts wore puggarees of blue cloth with white spots. The practise was never universal, however, and indeed many Boers merely believed that coloured hatbands provided the enemy with too tempting a target. Red was seldom used, as it was traditionally associated with the British military. At the start of the war some burghers wore ribbons with patriotic slogans on them – burghers on the southern front, for example, wore bands with '*Kaapstad of Bars!*' ('Cape Town or Die!'). In 1899, many burghers were issued with hat-badges depicting either the SAR or Free State coat of arms. Some of these may have been recycled from the stocks of the professional artillery units, while others appear to have been home made. They were usually worn on the turned-up brim of the hat – although again many burghers preferred not to do so. Similarly, some burghers liked to wear cockades, decorative badges made of coloured ribbons to denote their national allegiance – red/white/blue/orange/green for the Free State, and green/red/white/blue for the SAR. They were worn either on the hat or on the coat lapel. Many of the units of foreign volunteers who supported the Boer cause – but who fall outside the scope of this study – had a more professional approach to soldiering, and wore quasi-military uniforms of light-khaki hat, jacket and trousers.

The most obvious changes occurred in the burghers' weapons across the period. In the 1870s and 1880s, the commandos assembled with their own weapons. For the most part, as many observers noted, the burghers placed great store by their firearms, and whatever their failings in military style in other respects, they were usually armed with modern weapons in good condition. This reflected the fact that at that stage the Boer community was largely rural, and firearms were tools of daily survival. Lieutenant Newnham-Davis, a British officer stationed in the newly annexed Transvaal in 1877, recalled that:

> The stranger's rifle was always examined with interest, and if there was anything extraordinary in make or finish it was looked at with appreciation. And then probably the visitor asked to see the host's rifle, and the talk turned on buck-shooting. A Boer's rifle was his pet possession. It was to him what a favourite cue is to a professional

The German-made 7mm Mauser rifle, the principle weapon carried by the commandos in 1899. (Bill Cainan collection)

billiard player, what some especial gun is to a crack pigeon-shot. I shot in company with them time and again, and was always filled with admiration at the shooting they made at a galloping buck. A judgement in distance was a second nature to them.

Although a few burghers carried single-shot, percussion, rifled muzzle-loaders, which had been popular in the 1850s and 1860s, most by this time possessed single-shot breech-loaders. These included various models which were essentially breach-loading conversions of the old muzzle-loading patterns, such as the .577 calibre Snider, or the Westley-Richards 'Monkey Tail', whose quaint name was due to a curled lever which hinged upwards to open the breach. Such weapons fired lead bullets from greased paper cartridges, which had the great advantage that they could be made at home on the farm.

The most popular weapons of the period, however, were the breach-loading .577/.450 Martini-Henry and the .500/.450 Westley-Richards 'falling-block' rifle (known as the 'Free State Martini'). The Martini-Henry was the standard British infantry weapon of the period and, despite a slight tendency to overheat and a recoil which reflected its calibre, it was a solid, reliable, easy-to-use and accurate weapon which caused considerable damage to its target. The burghers equipped themselves with either the long rifles or the shorter carbine versions (easier to carry on horseback, but less accurate at a distance) according to taste and personal means. Both weapons fired bullets with metal (brass) cartridges which could hardly be home-made, but their expense was offset against a greater reliability and resistance to damp and damage.

Burghers armed with these weapons carried their cartridges in leather bandoliers which usually held 50 rounds in single loops. Fifty rounds represented considerable expenditure to an ordinary burgher, but some wealthier Boers wore two or even three bandoliers over their shoulders or around the waist. Such a load would, however, have been heavy and uncomfortable to wear for any length of time. Men armed with older pattern weapons wore cartridge boxes of various types, sometimes home made, or carried their rounds in their pockets.

Such was the reliability of the Martini-Henry that it was used throughout the 1880s and 1890s, and indeed when the SAR government decided to rearm in the aftermath of the Jameson Raid fresh supplies were ordered despite the fact it was outdated compared to magazine rifles firing smokeless charges. Nevertheless, the government was so impressed by the comparative merits of the German 7mm Mauser that in 1896 it ordered 25,000 Mausers and 10 million rounds of ammunition, and when these were tested they proved so popular that a further order was placed. Following the SAR's example, the Orange Free State also imported modern weapons in large quantities.

The Mauser was certainly an impressive weapon. Lightweight and accurate, it had an internal magazine which could be loaded with five rounds pressed from a clip into the breach from the top. A calm and experienced marksmen could produce a very high rate of accurate fire, while the smokeless propellant would not betray his position. The Mauser was available in a long rifle and carbine version, as well as various sporting models for those who preferred a more customised weapon. Rounds were usually carried in clips of five in leather bandoliers with either 10 or 12 clip-pouches. Because the Mauser rounds were significantly lighter than those of the Martini-Henry, individual burgers could carry more rounds with less discomfort. When war broke out in 1899, the SAR had some 37,100 Mausers, 31,600 Martini-Henrys, 4,750 Portuguese Guedes rifles, 2,340 British Lee-Metfords and 100 Krag Jorgensons. The Free State had 12,700 Mausers, 12,000 Martini-Henrys, 1,400 Guedes and 300 Lee-Metfords. Both republics also made an attempt to equip their small professional artillery units with modern Krupp, Creusot and Maxim-Nordenfeldt guns.

The new weapons were distributed to the commandos in late 1899. They were exchanged where possible for the weapons already owned by individual farmers. It is something of a myth, therefore, that the burghers of 1899 were highly experienced in the use of these weapons – many had fired only a few shots to test them before the war began. Johannes de Bruyn handed over his Martini-Henry, which had served him well at the battles of Laing's Nek, Majuba and Tshaneni with some reluctance. Nevertheless, the burghers were quick to appreciate the virtues of the new weapons, and within a few months the 7mm Mauser became an integral part of the commando way of life. A burgher named Van Wyk recalled that when the Mausers were issued:

> The majority were excited, angry at the *Rooinekke* ['red-necks' – British] and scathing about the moderates. They felt strong and confident, holding their power in their hands in the form of a Mauser and cartridges. A small group was gloomy [however], depressed. The weight of the Mauser and cartridges weighed heavily upon their shoulders, hearts and spirits. (p.82, Pretorius, 1999)

Although most of the firearms carried by the burghers throughout the period were equipped to carry bayonets, bayonet fighting was never

A group of burghers c.1900. One man (right) carries a Martini-Henry rifle, and another (second from left) a Mauser. The others have captured British Lee-Enfields.

practised by the Boers. Fighting at close quarters with the bayonet was the most challenging element of contemporary battle, and it required a high degree of emotional commitment and discipline to sustain an attack to close quarters and triumph in the visceral hand-to-hand fighting which ensued. Both concepts were essentially alien to the Boer approach to fighting, and while firefights at close quarters were common enough in 1899–1902, actual hand-to-hand fighting was rare.

BELIEF AND BELONGING

A common sense of identity and purpose was arguably the most important element in the morale of Boer commandos in the field throughout the nineteenth century. The individualistic nature of Boer society, the scattered nature of the farming community and the lack of focussed means to express intellectual concepts, meant that the burghers were not generally motivated by a theoretical sense of nationhood or by a political ideology. Since they were farmers not soldiers, they preferred not to fight at all, and only did so when they felt their everyday lives were under threat. Sometimes this threat was a local one – pressure from neighbouring African groups, for example – and sometimes it was perceived as all-consuming and immediate. The occupation of the Transvaal by the British in 1877 evoked memories of the unsympathetic treatment by the British administration on the Cape Frontier earlier in the century, and seemed to strike at the essential Boer need to run their affairs in their own way. In 1880 Johannes fought to overthrow British rule; in 1899 he fought to prevent the British imposing it again. At the very end of the Anglo-Boer War, a burgher named P.J. du Plessis explained his reasons for continuing to fight, even when the Boers were clearly defeated. 'We are not fighting for money,' he said. 'We are fighting only for freedom and the preservation of the two Republics! … one must have faith and an ideal, otherwise all this suffering is pointless.' A Joachim Potgieter simply observed that 'the Afrikaners have been truly aroused. Now is the time that we must and will get our independence.' (du Plessis p.329, Potgieter p.328, Pretorius, 1999).

Paradoxically, it was the sense of individuality which drew burghers together. There was none of the overt allegiance to military insignia or unit designations which was so carefully encouraged in regular armies of the time, and in fact many of the elements which defined Boer culture were by no means universal. It was a farming society in which not all those who fought were farmers, and individual needs sometimes overrode the common good. It was a society linked by a common language – Afrikaans – which in itself differed widely, from the near-Dutch used by the educated elite to the various rural dialects of the remote farming community.

Piet Bezeidenhout, a prominent burgher in the war of 1880–81. He wears a style of dress favoured by commandants in the early years – a frock coat and top hat – and is carrying a Westley-Richards 'falling-block' carbine.

Some elements of belief were sufficiently common to form unifying bonds, however. The Trek movement of the 1830s had been given spiritual cohesion by the commitment of the frontier communities to Lutheran Christian belief, and this was still common in the 1890s. As many as 80 per cent of the burghers in 1899 were members of the Dutch Reform Church. The DRC was characterised by a belief that the Bible was the only valid exposition of the will of God, and that God expected His followers to live their daily lives in accordance to its strictures. DRC services, conducted by ministers or *dominees*, were devout and lacking in pomp and ritual.

The DRC interpretation of Christian scripture provided many elements which encouraged a general sense of Boer nationalism. During the Great Trek, religious leaders had likened the Trekkers to the Children of Israel escaping persecution by migrating to the wilderness, and the idea that the Afrikaners were a chosen people survived across the century. This led many burghers to feel that their opponents were ungodly, and that they were fighting in a righteous cause. Jan Smuts, who emerged as one of the most successful guerrilla leaders of the 1899–1902 war, recalled that:

> When I joined the commandos in Natal I found a deeper feeling prevalent among the rank and file. No doubt there were braggarts and irresponsible featherheads, but the flower of the Boer army, the men who thought and felt deeply, the men who held the line of the Tugela, and to a large extent still continue in the field today, were actuated by vague but profound aspiration, to which expression was sometimes given in their prayers and religious services … As the contest has continued … and sorrow has followed sorrow until they seem verily to have arrived in the valley of the dark shadow, this remarkable faith in God and their destiny has become stronger.

Commandant Prinsloo of the Carolina commando put it more succinctly:

> I must say that never in my whole life have I felt the Hand of the Lord as clearly and palpably as during this … time I have been on commando. (p.172, Pretorius, 1999)

One manifestation of this belief was the sense that the Boer community was superior to the African societies among whom they lived. A comparatively small, scattered population, often under threat from African resistance, the Boers found solace in a sense of racial superiority which they justified through scripture. 'Our Constitution does not want any equality,' President Paul Kruger told the SAR *Volksraad* (Parliament) in 1879, 'and equality is also counter to the Bible, for social classes were instituted by the Lord.' This in itself justified the political expediency of reducing the power of African groups, depriving them of their land and exploiting their labour. Indeed, a sense of indignation that African groups were resisting the God-given order often pervades accounts of Boer campaigns against them, and found expression in occasional harsh treatment in the field.

Religious services were held regularly in the field in all campaigns. Some *dominees* accompanied the commandos themselves, but there were too few to administer to the spiritual needs of the entire army in 1899. More often, religious services were organised within each commando and were held by the commandant or by a respected elder. The services themselves were usually simple and heartfelt, with the burghers squatting or kneeling, bareheaded, on the open veldt. Individual religious commitment of course varied, and it is perhaps true that many of the urban, more sophisticated Boers were either ambivalent or simply disinterested. Among rural burghers – who remained the majority – however, it was quite literally an article of faith, and many read their Bibles on a daily basis, seeking solace and encouragement in the fight.

Such faith, too, ultimately made defeat easier to bare. At the end of the long guerrilla war in 1902, many burghers were only able to resign themselves to surrender in the belief that it was God's will. De Wet encouraged his men in the view that 'God willed it so – his name be praised.' De la Rey suggested that to continue the struggle when they were so obviously exhausted risked that will; 'Lord,' he said, '*thy* will be done – not my will to be the victor.' An ordinary burgher named P.J. Moller remarked that while the surrender was a terrible experience, 'I believe that this is God's way for our nation, [and] I want to submit, acquiesce in his will.' (p.343, Pretorius, 1999)

The unifying elements in Boer belief were not always sufficient to override the differences which came with an essentially local tradition, however. The individualistic outlook sometimes found expression in quarrels between commandants who refused to co-operate in the field, and it was not unknown for commandos to be reluctant to support those from other districts essentially local struggles. This was particularly true in expeditions against African enemies, when many burghers expressed a reluctance to risk their lives in quarrels which did not directly concern them.

At the outset of war in 1899, the relationship between Free State and Transvaal commandos was largely good, but this unity was seriously strained following the collapse of the conventional phase in early 1900 and the recriminations which ensued. In the subsequent guerrilla phase, commandos – with some exceptions – operated as much as possible within familiar areas and under the command of respected leaders. This mitigated against friction between commando groups, since they were no longer thrown together in the large armies which characterised the beginning of the war.

Most burghers, whatever their personal origins, were suspicious of the foreign volunteers who joined the Boer armies. Many of these volunteers were motivated by a passionate belief in the Boer cause and an

This British sketch, intended to portray the desperate plight of the 'bitter-enders', nonetheless reflects the real hardship many were reduced too: dressed in rags, and foraging for ammunition in deserted British camps.

antipathy towards British imperialism; they were prepared to share the Boers' hardships and risk injury, even death. Nevertheless, most burghers continued to look upon them as outsiders, and to question their motives, accepting their assistance only on the basis that it was freely given with no sense of obligation.

The attitudes towards the foreign volunteers in many ways epitomises the contradictions inherent in the Boer sense of self and belonging. The Boers fought not for a cause for its own sake, but for the survival of their lifestyle in the face of the alien and hostile world-view of outsiders. The logic of this approach ensured that when Boer society began to split in 1900 between 'hands-uppers' – those who surrendered to the British – and 'bitter-enders', those who continued in the struggle reserved particular contempt for members of their own community who had placed them so outside the boundaries of social acceptance as to reach accommodation with the British. Those Boers who subsequently joined units raised by the British – either in the hope of resolving the conflict, or of protecting their own farms – were liable to ruthless treatment if captured, and would remain social pariahs once the fighting ended.

LIFE ON CAMPAIGN

The war against the British in 1899–1902 was the most committed and prolonged campaign ever fought by burghers serving under the commando system. As such, it stretched an essentially short-term system beyond its limits, and produced significant changes in the nature of Boer military activity. While the early part of the war, despite the unprecedented numbers of burghers involved, remained in essence similar to the wars of the 1870s, 1880s and 1890s, the collapse of the Boer armies on all fronts from March 1900 threw the burghers onto the defensive and led to a prolonged guerrilla phase. This placed even greater emphasis on resilience, resourcefulness, and the sheer will to survive. In many ways, it was the guerrilla war which defined the burgher experience of the 1899–1902 conflict.

In February 1900 the British on the western front had relieved Kimberley and captured 4,000 men under General Piet Cronje at Paardeberg. Within days, Ladysmith on the Natal front had finally been relieved, and British troops began pushing back the Boer armies from their colonies, following them up into the republics. First the Free State capital, Bloemfontein, fell, then the SAR capital of Pretoria. The British offered amnesties to any Boer who surrendered, while the SAR government went into exile. The British felt the war was all but won.

In the aftermath of these catastrophic events, the fragile infrastructure which the republics had struggled to maintain to support their armies in the field collapsed. The cumbersome wagon trains which had characterised the advance into the British colonies just six months before began to disintegrate. Most of the African servants who had provided invaluable support in the conventional phase simply went home. Some of the more cumbersome artillery pieces were disabled and hidden so that the British might not find them.

So far from being defeated, however, the commandos emerged in a streamlined and more mobile form. While many of the elderly

commanders who had dominated the first phase retired from the war, a new, younger and more forceful generation came to the fore – men like Christiaan de Wet, Louis Botha, Jan Smuts and Koos de la Rey. A deliberate decision was taken to continue the struggle by guerrilla means and to utilise the Boer mastery of the countryside to strike at British supply columns, trains and rural garrisons, in the hope that by making the republics ungovernable the British would be forced eventually to reach a political accommodation.

The burghers never entirely abandoned their fondness for wagons, but the commandos of 1900–1902 were stripped of all but the barest necessity of vehicles. By the end of the war, some were entirely dependent on horses for all forms of transport. As such, they were far more mobile than the cumbersome British columns sent to pursue them. For the last two years of the war, the British strategy was dominated by the need to contain the commandos and destroy them by attrition. In this they were ultimately largely successful, and the lifestyle of men on commando was dominated by shortages and hardship.

One major difficulty was simply keeping men fed on commando. With no hope of supplies from the government, the burghers were entirely dependent on their own resources. For this reason, although they often undertook long-range expeditions – such as the various invasions of the northern Cape Colony, designed to encourage Afrikaners in the Cape to rise to support the republics – most commandos returned when they could to their home areas. These areas afforded them a secure support base which was invaluable in sustaining the war effort. Non-combatants who had remained on farms – old men, women, children and even those burghers who had officially surrendered – provided a clandestine source of farm produce such as cattle, wheat and rusks. Sometimes promissory notes were issued by the commandos to recompense the owners; often they were supplied as a patriotic contribution to the war effort. In some areas, despite the difficulties involved, this support continued to the very end of the war.

The British recognised the importance of this means of resupply, and adopted a very twentieth-century, counter-guerrilla means to combat it. In June 1900 the British commander-in-chief Lord Roberts announced

Burghers skirmishing with African warriors during the guerrilla phase. Although this picture is undoubtedly romanticised, African resistance to commando encroachments did increase as the war went on.

Johannes De Bruyn, c. 1881

A

The Battle of Laing's Nek, 28 February 1881

B

The Battle of Tshaneni, 5 June 1884

C

Johannes De Bruyn on the eve of the Anglo-Boer War, 1899

D

A Boer commando in the field during the Anglo-Boer War, 1899

E

Burghers at an evening meal, early 1900

F

"Bitter-enders' looting British weapons after a successful action, c.1901

G

The Battle of Holkrans, c. May 1902

H

that the farms of burghers known to still be under arms would be destroyed. From this point the British policy developed into one of 'scorched earth'. Initially specific farms were targeted, but as the fighting continued entire areas where commandos were known to operate were laid waste. Farm buildings were destroyed, livestock either killed or confiscated, and grain supplies burned. By early 1902 large areas of both republics, which had previously been among the most fertile, had been devastated. Chains of blockhouses were built across the veldt to limit the commandos' movements. Roland Schikkerling noted the awful effects of the continued struggle upon a civilian population:

'Bitter-enders' laying down their arms after the Peace of Vereeniging in May 1902. The boy sitting on the right, dressed in a blanket and battered hat, epitomises the plight of the last guerrilla groups at the end of the war; while there are a few Mausers in the pile of weapons, most are British weapons.

During our wanderings last night we stopped at a farmhouse to make some enquiry, but received scant courtesy from the woman in command. She approached, followed by a long diminishing file of children, the whole looking like a monstrous sea serpent, herself in the van forming the formidable head. With tearful fury she denounced us as thieves, drunkards, and cowards who, having left our manhood behind us in the big cities and other idolatrous centres, had come here to rob and ruin helpless Christian women and children, and to be instrumental in causing their homes to be burnt down, by drawing, through our uninvited presence, the enemy to their houses with fire and sword and, when he came, by by fleeing and leaving the distracted household to face him. The painful part of the reproach was the coarse grains of truth therein embedded. We admitted defeat and moved on.

For the most part, however, this policy failed to undermine support for the war. As Jan Smuts put it:

A weak man is broken by adversity; the sight of the ruin of his property and family is sufficient in most cases to utterly crush his spirit. On the other hand a brave and hardy spirit is braced by adversity – he does not sink hopelessly under calamities and wrongs; if he is really brave these will only nerve him to greater efforts.

The scarcity of food meant a greater dependence on biltong, while porridge made from crushed mealies generally replaced bread as a staple. Roland Schikkerling noted ruefully of mealies:

Take it away and we could not remain in the field ten days longer. Without it we would have had to abandon the war more than a year ago. A mealie cob should be on our coat of arms …

The British programme of destruction was unpopular with the men who carried it out, with the result that it was seldom entirely efficient.

Even in ruined farms commandos sometimes found vegetables, mealies or fruit trees that the soldiers had overlooked. At the start of the war cattle had been so plentiful in the farming community that it took a long time for the British to ravage the herds; and if meat could not be acquired from Boer supporters it could sometimes be traded or requisitioned from the African population. Some commandants relaxed the prohibition on shooting game – despite greater shortages of ammunition – and hunting became more widespread.

Indeed, success in the guerrilla phase often depended on the re-emergence of rural skills, and those commandos who included men who had been adept at survival in the veldt before the war coped best. Faced with chronic shortages of coffee, burghers learned to roast corn to produce an acceptable substitute, while a range of leaves were pressed into service as tobacco. Men who knew how to find bees' nests and extract honey became an important asset to any commando.

One important result of the scorched-earth policy was the impact on Boer civilian society. Initially, non-combatants made homeless by their farms being burnt were left to fend for themselves. Some attempted to find shelter and remain on their farms, but there was an underlying anxiety that they were vulnerable to attack by the African population. Many adopted a semi-nomadic lifestyle, trekking across the veldt from one source of food and succour to another, while others banded together into 'civilian laagers'. In an attempt to address this problem, the British began to round up civilians – mainly women and children – and establish them in concentration camps. Although these camps were intended primarily for their own protection, administrative inefficiency, poor facilities and lack of hygiene meant that disease took a heavy toll among those inside them. The heavy loss of life among women and children which resulted created a political scandal in Britain, and generated a legacy of bitterness among many Afrikaners which has lasted into recent times.

Most burghers in the field had felt the effect of shortages on their clothing long before the guerrilla war began. As the conventional phase dragged on, life in the veldt in all weathers began to take its inevitable toll on clothes and footwear. Within weeks some burghers complained of badly ripped clothes and battered footwear which could not easily be replaced from the erratic government supplies – and the situation would only get worse. Most burghers made their clothes last as long as possible by mending and patching, although as the fighting progressed material became short even for patches. Burghers covered tears with pieces cut from blankets or canvas from wagons, and then were forced to sew patches on their patches. When clothes gave way completely and a fresh supply could not be found, clothes were improvised from canvas wagon-tents, from tarpaulins, or from dressed animal hides. Home-made leather jackets and trousers became commonplace. Boots

Rural burghers in the 1881 war, armed with single-shot weapons with cartridges carried in satchels. Their practical outdoor clothes belied their military capabilities.

and shoes which finally fell apart were replaced by *velskoen* roughly cut from the hides of slaughtered cattle. Roland Schikkerling described a meeting with General Ben Viljoen and his commandants:

> The astonishing assemblage looked very much like a cannibal fancy-dress meeting. One officer wore a jacket of monkey skin, hair to the outside; another officer a jacket of leopardskin. One looked like a cross between Attila the Hun and Sancho Panza. Others wore odd garments of sheep, goat and deer skin, and of green baize and gaudily coloured kaffir blankets. Quite evidently the apparel does not here proclaim the man.

Similarly, the burghers clung to those tents and shelters they had been issued at the start of the war, and when these became worn or damaged beyond repair, they improvised shelters from looted tarpaulins or canvas, or whatever else came to hand. Some commandos, operating in familiar territory and out of sight of the British, erected temporary camps of huts made from branches and grass, while one commando operating near the eastern Transvaal goldfields lived for a while in corrugated-iron shelters made from sheeting found abandoned at the gold-workings.

In all things, their British enemy became a major source of resupply. By capturing supply convoys intended to feed British garrisons the guerrilla commandos not only inconvenienced the enemy but secured food for themselves. Luxuries were as sought after as staples – tinned meat, fruit preserves and jam, tobacco, sugar and coffee. If plates, cups, coffee pots and eating utensils were lost on commando, the best place to obtain new ones was from the British. In some areas, commandos took to shadowing British columns just to see what they could scavenge from their abandoned campsites.

The British, too, were a welcome source of clothing. Since the burghers had no real facilities for housing prisoners, they generally turned them loose, having first stripped them of their weapons and serviceable clothing. In most cases, the burghers simply ordered the British to undress, and offered their own rags in replacement. Occasionally prisoners objected to this treatment, but most regarded it with good humour. While the British were then faced with a long walk to the nearest garrison clad in battered civilian clothes, the burghers emerged in khaki jackets and trousers and army-issue boots.

This aspect of the war created some difficulty in itself. Throughout the war, the British adapted their uniforms to make them more suited to war in the veldt. In many units, sun-helmets gave way to slouch hats, and bandoliers gradually replaced ammunition belts. As the British therefore

Members of a Free State commando photographed c.1901. They are still carrying Mausers, but a number of men are wearing captured British uniforms. One man (second from left) still wears an OFS badge in the centre of his hat.

came to resemble the general appearance of the Boers, the Boers became more dependent on captured British uniforms. It became increasingly difficult to tell the two armies apart. Usually, the burghers removed conspicuous British insignia so that they would not be mistaken for the enemy, but some did not see the need, while in a few cases insignia were deliberately retained to confuse the British. When reports of this practise reached the British, they ordered that Boers captured in British uniforms should be shot. Although only small numbers of executions did take place, the practice was never entirely abandoned.

Indeed, towards the end of the war, some commandos – including Jan Smuts – deliberately adopted a quasi-military air of discipline and appearance which bolstered them against the increasingly rigorous role they had to play. In such commandos captured British jackets, trousers and even riding boots were worn without insignia but with a sense of purpose reflecting a professionalism which had grown out of years of hardship and fighting.

Horses, too, were an invaluable form of loot. While the thorough-breds brought out by British cavalry regiments were of limited use to the Boers, many colonial units had equipped themselves with local horses, and these were in great demand as death and injury reduced the Boers' stock. It was in the matter of weapons, however, that the burghers most came to depend upon the British. Whatever the merits of the Mauser, the burghers nonetheless respected the Lee-Metford and Lee-Enfield rifles which were standard issue among British troops. Indeed, the respective advantages of the two weapons in terms of weight, range and accuracy were hard to resolve, and the Mauser's only real benefit lay in the fact that it was quicker to reload in the heat of action – five rounds could be loaded in one movement from a clip, whereas the Lee-Metford's magazine had to be reloaded with individual rounds. The supply of Mausers was, however, finite, for early in the war the British entered into an accord with the Portuguese government to prevent goods entering the republics via Mozambique. When the British captured quantities of Boer weapons, they destroyed them and although some enterprising artisans specialised in restoring burnt weapons, the supply of rifles steadily dwindled, while expended ammunition could not easily be replaced. In the guerrilla phase, it was not unusual for burghers carrying Mausers to go into action with just a handful of cartridges. From the very beginning of the war, however, the burghers captured British firearms and ammunition whenever they were successful in action – at the Battle of Nicholson's Nek, outside Ladysmith, in October 1899 the Boers captured over 1,000 Lee-Metfords and 20 cases of ammunition alone – these weapons were largely used to replace outdated Martini-Henrys in Boer hands. By the time the guerrilla war was under way in earnest, the habit of exploiting captured British weapons had long been established. With each fresh success, more British rifles found their way into Boer hands, and as lack of ammunition increasingly rendered the Mausers useless, so they were replaced by Lee-Metfords.

The Anglo-Boer War was not, of course, waged in an empty landscape. For the most part, the commandos used areas farmed by fellow Afrikaners as a support base, but these areas were deliberately targeted for reprisals by the British, forcing the commandos to range further afield. This meant that they were sometimes obliged to move through areas with a high level of African settlement.

The relationship between the combatants and the African population of southern Africa during the war was complex. Both sides maintained the myth that it was a 'white man's war' – even though the Boers employed thousands of African servants during the conventional phase, while the British relied increasingly on armed black scouts during the guerrilla phase. The reaction of ordinary African societies was mixed, however. Commandos operating in the Eastern Free State found a ready source of food and blankets among the BaSotho, until the British sealed off the BaSotholand border. In the SAR and Natal, however, many African groups displayed a latent hostility towards the commandos. This reflected both political pragmatism – a feeling that the British would eventually win the war, and that political advantages would flow from allying themselves with the winner – and long-standing resentment of Boer territorial ambitions. In the eastern SAR the Boers were surrounded by an arc of peoples with whom they had been in conflict between 1876 and 1899 – the Venda, Pedi and Transvaal Ndebele. Further east, in Zululand, the British used their influence over the Zulu Royal House to limit Boer incursions into Zulu territory.

As the effects of the scorched-earth policy began to be felt, many commandos felt they had little alternative but to forage for food supplies among the various African groups. By the middle of 1900, many of those groups were inclined to resist, and the burghers faced increasing hostility and even attacks when they operated in such areas. They often reacted harshly under such circumstances, intimidating black communities who had turned against them or were suspected of supporting the British.

By far the most serious incident occurred on the night of 6 May 1902, near Johannes' farm outside Vryheid. This area had been the subject of considerable friction between the Zulu kingdom and the SAR in the 1870s; in 1884 it had been ceded to those Boers who had supported the royalist faction in the Zulu civil war. Considerable tension remained, however, between the Afrikaner community and the most powerful local group, the abaQulusi. Although the British had occupied the town of Vryheid, the Vryheid and Utrecht commandos had been operating in the area in April 1902, and augmenting their supplies from well-wishers in the rural community by looting from the abaQulusi. Although Afrikaner histories describe what happened next as an unprovoked attack amounting to murder, the abaQulusi remain adamant to this day that they were provoked – their herds were stolen, herdsmen shot dead and Zulu homesteads burned. The abaQulusi complained to the British

In order to destroy the guerrillas' source of supply, the British waged a scorched-earth policy, destroying farms, livestock and crops. 'Removing a Boer family from a farm on the Vaal', 1900. (National Army Museum)

garrison in Vryheid, who were reluctant to intervene because an armistice had been declared. When the Boer commandant heard of the abaQulusi complaints, he dismissed the Zulus as 'chicken lice'. Just before dawn on 6 May, while the Boers were camped below a hill known as Holkrans, an impi of up to 1,000 Zulu surrounded and attacked them. The loss of life was heavy on both sides: 100 Zulus were killed or injured and 53 of the 76 Boers killed.

The action at Holkrans was a significant indication of the growing hostility of African groups towards the commandos, and it played an important role in shaping Boer attitudes in the negotiations which finally brought the war to a close.

EXPERIENCE OF BATTLE

A number of factors shaped the Boer response to the testing military challenges of the period 1876–1902. The individualism inherent in Boer society, the varying perception at different times of the threat to their way of life, an awareness of their battlefield strengths combined with an unwillingness to risk unnecessary loss of life, all combined to produce differing reactions under particular circumstances.

The greatest battlefield advantages possessed by the burghers were the accuracy of their firepower, their horsemanship and mobility, and their instinctive understanding of terrain. Properly exploited, these could be a devastating combination.

The 1881 campaign perhaps showed these elements to best effect when employed against a well-armed and professional army. Boer tactics were often defensive, simply because the burghers recognised that the easiest way to defeat an enemy with minimum cost to themselves was to lure him into a costly attack on selected ground exposed to their firepower. This was a tactical lesson which had been learned in Voortrekker battles against African enemies, such as Vechtkop (1836) and Ncome/Blood River (1838), and which had become a fundamental part of Boer military thinking. Clearly, the wagon laagers of old were outmoded in the face of an enemy armed with equally efficient modern weapons – as Paardeberg would prove – and instead the burghers relied on trenches as a means of defence during static periods on campaign.

At their simplest, these trenches were shallow scrapes in the ground, with the dislodged boulders piled up in front. This was sufficient to shelter a crouching or lying man against return fire. Trenches were not dug in continual lines, but were

The wagon laager had evolved on the Cape Frontier, and was an effective method of defence against an enemy armed with close-combat weapons – such as the Zulu, as here.

usually intended to shelter ten or 20 men, and were carefully placed to provide overlapping fields of fire. The choice of ground was an important element in the building of trenches. When Johannes de Bruyn first saw action at Laing's Nek in January 1881, he fought from a shallow trench built on the forward slope of a hill; his position commanded a killing ground of about 80 yards in front of him, beyond which the ground dropped away, so that his position was largely invisible to his enemy until they emerged from the dead ground for their final approach. In 1899, on the Kimberley front, the burghers built a complex of trenches along the foot of the Magersfontein ridge in a position which deceived the British, who expected them to fortify the higher ground.

If there was sufficient time and manpower – particularly the services of African labourers – the burghers often built quite extensive fortifications. On the Ladysmith front in 1899, where the ground was hard and rocky, they built stout stone sangars across the front of their positions to compensate for the lack of depth. At Magersfontein, however, where the soil was sandy and less rocky, many Boers built deep trenches which contained hollowed-out bomb-shelters, or sometimes cut firing steps or seats into the walls to make themselves comfortable.

Despite the security they afforded, few burghers relished fighting from trenches. In both 1881 and 1899 the British preceded their attacks on Boer positions with heavy artillery bombardments. Johannes was not alone in never having heard the sound of a shell exploding before his experience of battle at Laing's Nek – the loudest sounds he had ever heard up until then were natural ones, like the sharp crack of thunder that accompanied the summer storms on the high veldt. When the first shells exploded nearby, preceding the British assault, he was terrified by the whine which gave a split second's warning of the approaching shell, by the sudden crack of the explosion and by the way the ground was torn up all around by the shrapnel balls scattered by the air burst. Burghers injured by shellfire suffered appalling injuries which were deeply shocking to men for whom the tasks of slaughtering animals for meat, or an occasional accident on the farm, had served as poor preparation for the realities of

The practical defensive value of the laager was limited in campaigns against an enemy armed with modern weapons, as this photograph depicting the interior of Cronje's laager at Paardeberg, after his surrender in February 1900, suggests.

Despite its limitations, the laager remained the preferred method of preparing a camp even during the guerrilla war of 1900-02.

battle. Johannes had by no means lost this fear of artillery when he faced it again in 1899, and indeed on that occasion it seemed even more terrifying due to the widespread use of new lyddite charges in British shells. The British guns in 1899 were heavier than in 1881, and lyddite exploded with a more terrifying crash, leaving heavy, yellow, sulphurous smoke in the air which caught the throat and burned the eyes. At first, many burghers thought lyddite fumes were poisonous, but once they began to realise that trenches were an effective shelter against shellfire, and that the gases were no more than an irritant, they began to lose some of their fear of bombardment. Indeed, in the trenches along the Thukela line, outside Ladysmith, Johannes saw many burghers react to British shellfire with remarkable nonchalance. One elderly burgher steadfastly read his Bible throughout a barrage without looking up, while on one occasion young *penkoppe* dared one another to stand on the parapet, and only drop into cover at the last moment as they heard the shell approach.

Although in most campaigns of the period the burghers had limited access to artillery of their own, their main response on the battlefield relied on small-arms fire.

A lyddite shell exploding on a Boer position at Spion Kop, January 1900. The experience of being under shellfire was an intimidating one when burghers first experienced it, but in fact it was seldom as effective as this drawing suggests.

The burghers were in effect instinctive mounted infantry, who used the horse to move rapidly from one part of the battlefield to another, then dismounted to fight on foot. In 1881 Johannes had fought with a Martini-Henry rifle, and had been impressed with its accuracy and reliability. Like his colleagues, no one had taught him musketry drill – he simply relied on the skills as a marksman he had learned on the farm. At Laing's Nek, no one had directed his fire, beyond an admonition to wait until the enemy were in range. After that, he simply picked his own target, aimed and fired when ready – an experience which was overwhelmingly typical of Boer marksmanship in the field. He was undoubtedly a good shot, although what made his fire so deadly was not so much an unnatural skill as an experience in handling his weapon, in judging distance and anticipating the speed of a moving target. In 1881 and again in 1899, his British opponents had spent little time on musketry exercises, and had then largely been trained to fire at static targets over fixed distances.

For many burghers, in the excitement of the moment, the act of shooting became almost automatic. J.H. Meyer, a burgher who fought at Modder River, recalled the intensity of his emotional responses:

> In dead silence, peering fixedly ahead, we lie waiting. All at once I see them, thousands of them. Like a swarm of locusts they come pouring over the hills. It is a broad, solid host of marching infantry and mounted divisions – Methuen's ten thousand. The morning sun sparkles on a huge sea of glinting rifle barrels.

Perfectly in step they march and ride … It is spectacular, and terrifying. Resolutely, ineluctably, they advance straight at us … two thousand yards, fifteen hundred, one thousand, eight hundred. 'Wait til four hundred yards, that's orders', my pal Jerry Basson, lying next to me, whispers. Four hundred yards against this fearful horde of soldiers! It's madness, sheer madness! It echoes inside my brain. I shake like a reed and sweat beads on my forehead … I lie with my finger quivering on my trigger, not knowing where to aim. There are too many of them … The tension is unbearable … Now I am the consummate killer that every man becomes on the battlefield: calculating, cold-blooded. Gone is the tension, the terrible fear that gripped me a moment ago. Now I am deadly calm, and with deadly calm I pick my man, pick them one by one. I pick him, my Mauser drops, my left eye closes, I get him in my sights and my Mauser cracks. The Englishman totters, drops his rifle, grabs his chest, staggers, stumbles forward, drops to his knees, rolls over, lies there. I shoot them down, one after another. (p.137, 139, Pretorius, 1999)

When fighting against an enemy equipped only with close-combat weapons, the burghers' skill with rifles was decisive and difficult to counter. When Johannes fought at the Battle of Tshaneni in 1884, supporting the royalist uSuthu faction against the anti-royalist Mandlakazi, he saw for himself the devastation even single-shot breach-loaders like the Martini-Henry could cause. The Mandlakazi, attacking in the open, were shot down in large numbers with little hope of reply, by Boers firing from horseback over the heads of the uSuthu. This battle, in many respects, was an indication that the burghers possessed a military technology which was unbeatable in a purely African context; on rare occasions when African enemies did triumph at close quarters, such as at Holkrans, they were forced to rely on surprise and the cover of darkness to minimise the danger of Boer rifle fire.

The potential of Boer firepower, moreover, was only increased with the widespread use of the Mauser in 1899. Not only was it possible to fire at a much faster rate, due to the bolt action and magazine, but the smokeless propellant produced only the thinnest cough of smoke, compared to the dense clouds produced by the old single-shot breach-loaders. At Laing's Nek and Tshaneni Johannes had seen the enemy obscured by smoke just minutes after the battle began, and he and his colleagues had had to snatch their targets where they appeared briefly in the gloom. When he fought later at Colenso, Johannes

Throughout the period, the burghers were most effective on the battlefield when they were able to exploit their formidable firepower from the protection of trenches or natural features.

had been amazed to see that the devastating fire produced by hundreds of burghers in the trenches produced hardly any smoke at all. Indeed, those burghers who still carried a Martini-Henry soon became unpopular on commando, as the smoke from their rifles was the only thing liable to give away their positions.

Johannes shot down three or perhaps four Zulus at Tshaneni and the subsequent pursuit. He felt little compunction in killing African enemies, and approached the task with an emotional detachment akin to his hunting experiences. He had felt very different at Laing's Nek, however, when he had first shot at a white man and seen him fall. Wandering over the killing ground in front of his trench after the battle, he was appalled at the destruction wrought by Boer fire. The heavy Martini-Henry bullets caused significant tissue damage at close range, and the sight of the pale faces of the British dead, clotted and splashed with blood, was deeply disturbing. Johannes had often heard British troops described as *roinekke* – rednecks – from the way their necks burned when they were first in the African sun. At Laing's Nek he couldn't resist seeing if this story was true, and gently lifted the sun-helmet from across the face of a fallen soldier to look. The sight of a gaping exit wound in the man's head made Johannes physically sick.

Johannes never entirely lost his feeling of remorse at killing British troops. While some of his colleagues became hardened to war and indifferent, and a few nursed a deep hatred of the enemy born of the policy of farm-burning and the death of loved ones in the concentration camps, Johannes and many like him always felt a sense of remorse at killing a foe who, like themselves, were white-skinned and Christian. Although in the heat of battle Johannes never questioned the necessity, once the shooting had stopped he felt only compassion for the fallen, and always did what he could to succour the wounded. Johannes saw for himself the aftermath of the awful destruction at Spion Kop, arguably the most concentrated killing ground experienced by any burgher – 'The field of battle was horrible,' wrote one journalist. 'Men were literally blown to pieces by shellfire. I counted thirteen heads blown from bodies, some wholly, others from the ears upwards, and so on' – and shared Commandant Hendrik Prinsloo's regret that 'It seems a pity that we, belonging to two God-fearing nations, should kill one another like that.' One elderly burgher, looking at the huddled British dead, was heard to murmur simply, 'Poor lads, poor lads'. Surveying the British dead lying out in the sun after the Battle of Magersfontein, one burgher observed that 'There lies our enemy, and behind our lines there is no rejoicing about the splendid victory but rather a conspicuous silence at the horror of it.' (p.153, Pretorius, 1999)

After the Battle of Nicholson's Nek, Deneys Reitz of the Pretoria commando recalled that 'Dead and wounded soldiers lay all around, and the cries and groans of agony, the dreadful sights, haunted me for many a day, for though I had seen death by violence of late, there had been nothing to approach the horrors accumulated there.'

The experience of being under fire was equally disturbing. At first Johannes was unnerved by the spitting noise bullets made as they passed close by and the crack of rounds shattering on boulders; like many of his colleagues he gave way to a feeling that he was being singled out as a particular target. With experience, however, he came to realise that luck

Impressive Boer stoneworks protecting a field gun on the heights overlooking the Colenso battlefield. On the boulder-strewn Natal front, rocks were often used by the burghers to improvise breastworks.

In 1899 both the SAR and OFS maintained small regular artillery formations. The guns played an important role during the conventional phase, but many – like this 155mm 'Long Tom', drawn by oxen – were destroyed at the beginning of the guerrilla war. (Ron Sheeley)

largely determined his fate, and he placed his faith in the Lord to deliver him from harm. That sense that his life was in the hands of a higher power stayed with him throughout his military experiences, and remained a lasting comfort.

The loss of a friend or comrade was nevertheless keenly felt. The burghers lacked discipline of professional armies which served to bolster morale in the face of heavy casualties. Deneys Reitz, scrambling up the steep slopes of Spion Kop to attack the British entrenched at the top, recalled his horror at passing dead comrades along the way:

I soon came upon the body of John Malherbe, our Corporal's brother, with a bullet between his eyes; a few paces further lay two more dead men of our commando. Further on I found my tent-mate, poor Robert Reinecke, shot through the head, and not far off L. de Villiers of our corporalship lay dead. Higher up was Krige, another of Isaac's men, with a bullet through both lungs, still alive, and beyond him Walter de Vos of my tent shot through the chest, but smiling cheerfully as we passed. Apart from the Pretoria men there were many dead and wounded, mostly Carolina burghers from the eastern Transvaal … Half-way acoss lay the huddled body of a dead man and now that I had time to look more carefully at him I recognised Charles Jeppe, the last of my tent-mates. His death keenly affected me for we had been particularly good friends.

Johannes de Bruyn had no concept of dying for glory, and saw no dishonour in retreat before the enemy. Once a position had become too dangerous, he regarded it as only sensible to abandon it and take up a fresh one elsewhere. The Boers lived to fight another day; reckless exposure to danger merely left loved ones to fend for themselves alone on the farm.

On occasion, this could lead to a lack of aggressive spirit in the field, particularly in wars against African enemies where the chance of victory in battle seemed slim, and the issues at stake insufficient to encourage risks. During the campaign against King Sekhukhune of the Pedi in 1876, the Pedi retired before the Boer advance and took up positions on rocky hillsides protected by stone walls. To drive them out would have required a determined assault and resulted in heavy loss of life, and this the burghers refused to entertain. Instead, they left the assault to their African allies – a contingent of Swazis – but refused to support their attack. The Swazis became so disillusioned that they abandoned the campaign, and it was left to the burghers to establish a chain of forts around Sekhukhune's territory in an effort to contain the Pedi. Significantly, the Pedi were finally defeated by a combined British and Swazi assault in late 1879.

Where African enemies took refuge in strongholds, the burghers usually preferred to isolate and starve them into submission. In 1894 the SAR subdued some 400 men of the Hanawa who had defended the Blouberg mountain for several months; the burghers eventually triumphed by destroying the Hanawa huts and crops, cutting them off from their water supplies – methods which, ironically, foreshadowed British scorched-earth techniques a few years later. In the campaigns against the Transvaal Ndebele, who had secured themselves in caves and crevices in the mountains of the eastern Transvaal, the burghers used explosives to seal up the caves and suppress resistance.

In the event of a failure of will in battle, there was little recourse available to commando leaders. A few were known to use their *sjamboks* to encourage men out of cover in the heat of the action, while others relied on the more effective power of their personalities. If the burghers simply chose not to obey, however, there was nothing to be done. Individual failures of courage were also regarded leniently; on more than one occasion between 1899 and 1902 Johannes heard burghers declare simply, 'It's too dangerous for me here; I won't stay to be shot', before falling back to a safer position. Men who were consistently unwilling to take part in dangerous attacks were, however, usually ordered to look after the horses – an important duty which nonetheless exposed their colleagues to less danger from their personal failings.

Not that the burghers could not mount extremely effective assaults when they were sufficiently motivated. At the Battle of Schuinshoogte (Ingogo), where a small British force was isolated on a rocky rise, the burghers gradually surrounded the British position by stalking them on foot from rock to rock, gradually working round their flanks and advancing to within easy rifle range. From secure positions themselves, the burghers picked off conspicuous targets – including British gunners – and kept the remainder pinned down; only the onset of darkness allowed the survivors to escape.

The climactic battle of the 1881 campaign, Majuba, demonstrated the most successful elements of Boer offensive tactics. Initially disconcerted to find that the

The Battle of Majuba in February 1881 – the climactic battle of the Transvaal Rebellion. The battle demonstrated the burghers' ability to skirmish in attack to good effect. (MuseumAfrica)

British had occupied Majuba hill overnight, a position which overlooked their trenches, the burghers responded to the exhortations of their commandants that the war might be lost if they did not counter-attack immediately. They skirmished up the steep slopes of the hill in small groups, one covering another as they went by firing at the soldiers silhouetted on the skyline above. Johannes himself, along with many of his younger colleagues, was among the attacking party, pulling himself up by tufts of grass, and ducking among the cliffs and boulders which broke the ascent, while older men like his father fired over their heads from below. Years later, Johannes witnessed a similar yet more desperate assault on Spion Kop, where a determination to hold the Thukela line at all costs led burghers to advance to within feet of the British positions. The climax of both battles was a desperate firefight behind boulders at close range, with men wriggling down as tightly as they could between the rocks and exchanging fire at a few yards' – or even feet – range. As Deneys Reitz recalled of Spion Kop:

> The English troops lay so near that one could have tossed a biscuit tin among them, and whilst the losses which they were causing us were only too evident, we on our side did not know that we were inflicting even greater damage upon them. Our own casualties lay hideously among us, but theirs were screened from view behind the breastwork.

Actual hand-to-hand fighting was rare, as the burghers shied away from the brutal nature of killing at close quarters. The British, whose troops were trained in bayonet fighting, often sought to close with the Boers, but it was unusual for their charges to strike home. Often, they suffered such heavy casualties on the approach that the attack simply collapsed, or sometimes the charge lost momentum and a firefight developed. Where a charge did strike home, the burghers often abandoned their position at the last minute, retiring as quickly as they could on their horses and retreating to fight another day. On those occasions when burghers did stand their ground, they met British bayonets with close-range shooting or with clubbed rifles. Reitz again, describing an attack on a British camp at Nooitgedacht on 13 December 1900:

> Almost before we knew it, we were swarming over the walls, shooting and clubbing in hand-to-hand conflict. It was sharp work. I have a confused recollection of fending bayonet thrusts and firing point-blank into men's faces; then of soldiers running to the rear or putting up their hands, and as we stood panting and excited within the barricades, we could scarcely believe that the fighting was won.

All attacks depend on an element of co-ordination which did not always come naturally to burghers in the field, and they often relied instead on the determination of the moment. When General I.S. Ferriera asked a burgher named Izak Meyer of the Ladybrand commando what his most important lesson in war had been, Meyer replied 'To look back!' – to make sure that his colleagues were still following him! During

A British sketch purporting to depict a charge by British lancers from the Boer perspective. Despite the obvious propaganda element, the picture does demonstrate the different attitudes to hand-to-hand combat among the respective combatants. The Boers were not trained in the use of edged weapons, and sought to avoid them where they could.

the guerrilla phase, however, many commandos developed the tactic of launching mounted attacks. By that stage, many burghers were veterans of numerous fights and skirmishes, and had learnt some of the practical techniques of soldiering by experience. Attacks on horseback in the open could be extremely vulnerable to return fire if the enemy were expecting them, but in the wide-ranging hit-and-run war of 1901-02 it was often possible for commandos to launch surprise attacks on British convoys. A sudden dash across the veldt, firing from the saddle, could be both exhilarating for participants and intimidating for the enemy. Sometimes, if the enemy failed to form up, the charge carried right through the British positions; occasionally, if the enemy responded with return fire, the burghers would rein in close to the enemy, jump off their horses, and continue the advance on foot.

When burghers were killed and it was possible to recover their bodies, they were usually given a simple burial in the field with a service attended by their colleagues. Burghers had few qualms about abandoning their dead to the British, as they knew they would invariably receive a Christian burial, but there was a marked reluctance to abandon casualties to African enemies. Not only might bodies be mutilated, but they would not receive appropriate funeral rites. If bodies could not be recovered in action without risk, it was not unusual to seek out remains days or even months later. Many burghers buried in the field were exhumed after the fighting and the bodies returned to family farms. A lot of isolated graves from the 1899–1902 conflict were later opened and the remains collected together for burial in appropriate plots.

In most of the campaigns of the period, the burghers relied on civilian medical support to treat injury or sickness. Civilian doctors – usually from the commandos' home districts – accompanied them in 1881, in the African wars of the 1890s, and again in 1899–1902. In 1899, government-sponsored medical facilities were understaffed and could not meet the needs of the mobilised republican armies. They were, however, supported by nine foreign ambulances, sponsored by overseas Red Cross agencies. For the most part, the foreign ambulances were staffed by well-trained doctors and nurses, and were well equipped. The ambulances themselves were light horse- or mule-drawn wagons, which, despite the best intentions of the staff, offered the prospect of an agonising journey over the rocky veldt to the field hospitals which had been set up in tents near the main laagers. As the war progressed, however, the dispersal of the commandos inevitably meant that they often functioned without much hope of trained medical help.

In any case, since the republics lacked a trained stretcher-bearer corps, there were seldom appointed personnel to carry wounded men out of the front line to the hospital quarters, and burghers usually relied on the help of their comrades. In the Mmalebogo campaign of 1894, the Rev. Rae recalled how two men, wounded in action, had to be sent back to the laager to be treated, their 'wounds … bound up with torn handkerchiefs obtained from their comrades'. Rae noted that many burghers were sceptical of the treatment proffered by trained doctors, especially if it involved the loss of a limb. 'The doctor's opinion was never regarded nor his advice accepted among the Boers; the amputation was almost in every case postponed until it was too late to do any good.' In his opinion, however, 'everything possible was being done to alleviate the sufferings of the wounded'.

If proper medical facilities were not available, the burghers had to rely on their own resilience, or the compassion of the enemy. Farm life had accustomed many rural burghers to endure unexpected accidents, and on campaign the burghers were at risk not only from enemy action but from the dangers of life on the veldt itself – falls from horses, snake-bite, even lightning strikes. Some burghers were adept at home-made remedies or at binding up broken limbs, while there are occasional references to toughened farmers performing minor surgery on themselves. Perhaps the most famous incident occurred to the young Paul Kruger, whose thumb was shattered when his gun exploded on a remote hunting expedition. With only his family to aid him:

> I took my knife, intending to perform the operation, but they took it away from me. I got hold of another a little later and removed as much as was necessary. The worst bleeding was over, but the operation was a very painful one. I had no means of deadening the pain, so I tried to persuade myself that the hand on which I was performing this surgical operation belonged to somebody else. This wound healed very slowly. The women sprinkled finely-powdered sugar on it, and from time to time, I had to remove the dead flesh with my pocket knife; but gangrene set in after all. Different remedies were employed, but all seemed useless, for the black marks rose as far as the shoulder. Then they killed a goat, took out the stomach and cut it open. I put my hand into it while it was still warm. This Boer remedy succeeded for, when it came to the turn of the second goat, my hand was already easier and the damage much less. The wound took over six months to heal.

That this was not an isolated incident is testified by an anecdote from Sir Arthur Cunynghame, the British commander at the Cape in the mid-1870s, who saw a burgher with a similar injury directing his son in 'shaping off' his damaged fingers with a hammer and chisel.

By the 1890s, medical science had developed to a degree that effective medicines – particularly anaesthetics, such as chloroform – were more readily available. These, like almost everything else that sustained the burghers from 1900 to 1902, were often captured from the British. Nevertheless, during the guerrilla phase, the most reliable means of treating men wounded in an unsuccessful action was simply to leave them on the field for the enemy to find. The British could generally be relied upon to offer them treatment from their far more extensive medical facilities.

AFTERMATH

Johannes de Bruyn's early military experience left him largely unscathed and triumphant. The war of 1881 caused the British to revoke their annexation of the Transvaal, and Johannes shared the general sense of euphoria which characterised the dissolution of the commandos and their return home. In 1884, his adventure in Zululand had seen him rewarded with a farm of his own, and a role as a founding father of the New Republic.

In 1902, however, his ex-periences were very different. He served with the Vryheid commando from the start of the war, through the conventional phase – including the bitter fighting around Ladysmith – and then the long guerrilla campaign. He had seen many of his colleagues killed and others captured, to be deported overseas to prison camps elsewhere in the British Empire, such as Ceylon or St Helena. He had seen the indomitable spirit of the commandos gradually worn down by the British war of attrition, and he had been forced in the end to accept the inevitability of defeat. When he finally laid down his arms in the general surrender at the end of May 1902, he hardly recognised himself from the man who had ridden out over two long years before. He was spare, weather-beaten, long haired and bearded, and apart from his rough *velskoen* he was clad entirely in clothes of British origin; the rifle he surrendered was a British Lee-Metford. For many, the surrender did indeed seem the bitterest of ends. Izak Meyer recalled the desolation of that moment:

General Piet Cronje and his wife and guard during their confinement on the island of St Helena. Cronje surrendered at Paardeberg in February 1900; his African servants accompanied him into exile. (Ron Sheeley)

> And now the end has come, now they have to lay down their arms and bow before the enemy. Silently they stand in line. Together with Commandant Kirsten I walk past them, these comrades of mine who have fought and suffered with me. I see the look in their eyes. I read their minds. I feel the tension, bitterness, anger, rebellion raging inside them. (p.344, Pretorius, 1999)

While for De Wet:

> This surrender was no more and no less than the sacrifice of our independence. I have often been at the death-bed and of the burial of those who have been nearest to my heart – father, mother, brother and friend – but the grief which I felt on those occasions was not to be compared with what I now underwent at the burial of my Nation!

For some, the oath of allegiance which the burghers were required to sign as part of the surrender agreement was too much to bare.

When Deneys Reitz surrendered:

> our men fired away their ammunition into the air, smashed their rifle butts and sullenly flung their broken weapons down before putting their names to the undertaking which each man was called upon to sign, that he would abide by the peace terms. When my father's turn came, he handed over his rifle, but refused to sign … The officer pointed out that he would not be allowed to remain in the country, and my father agreed … I had to stand by him, so I also refused to sign.

A Boer family returning to their boarded-up farm at the end of hostilities. This picture celebrates the relief that the war was at last over; in fact, many burghers returned to find their farms in ruins. (MuseumAfrica)

Some, like the Reitz family, went into exile. Most, like Johannes de Bruyn, returned to their farms to find the buildings gutted by fire, the roofs missing, and weeds growing through the hard-earth floors. The skulls and long-bones of his cattle, slaughtered by the British, still lay strewn across the veldt, and several Zulu families had moved onto outlying parts of his land. George Mossop who, like Johannes, had won his farm near Vryheid as a reward for taking part in the Tshaneni commando, suffered the same experience, his farm being destroyed during his absence by one side or the other:

> When the war ended I found that all I possessed had gone up in flames and smoke, leaving me sitting on the ashes … Selecting a comfortable seat in a heap of burnt and twisted corrugated iron between four blackened walls, with big gaps in them where at one time they boasted windows and doors – in the days of my respectability it was my dining room – I reviewed my position. 'Well, so this is this, thirteen thousand pounds gone in one bang! And the bales of wool in the big shed were worth all of two thousand.'

Like Mossop, the war had impoverished Johannes, but he was young and resilient enough to start again. In the post-war years, the British government offered subsidies to the defeated republics to repair some of the damage done by the scorched-earth policies. Johannes eventually rebuilt his farm, though many of his colleagues were not so fortunate. Once the war was over the British released their prisoners, but not all returned to South Africa, preferring instead to build new lives elsewhere rather than live under British rule. Others returned home to find their farms destroyed and their families dead in the concentration camps. The war created a class of 'poor whites' who drifted to the towns and accelerated the slow urbanisation of Afrikaner society. Within a decade the old republics and former British colonies were linked together for the first time as the Union of South Africa. The aspirations of the black Africans who had supported the British between 1899 and 1902 were largely sacrificed in an attempt to reconcile the divided white population. Nonetheless, those divisions, not only between Afrikaners and English-

speaking South Africans but also between 'hands uppers' and 'bitter-enders' within Afrikaner society continued to dominate politics into the post colonial period. The bitterness felt by many of the Boer veterans of 1899–1902 endured and found expression in an intense form of Afrikaner nationalism which would shape the history of South Africa throughout much of the twentieth century.

In June 1900 the British offered an amnesty to Boers who wished to lay down their arms. Here burghers surrender their weapons and take the 'oath of neutrality'. Many did indeed abandon the struggle; some later returned to join the commandos, while others opted to fight in units like the National Scouts, raised by the British.

MUSEUM COLLECTIONS

The Anglo-Boer War of 1899–1902 led to the greatest commitment of troops from the British Army of any of the Victorian colonial wars. As a result, most of the regimental museums in the UK have some material relating to the war – often including captured Boer items. The biggest collection, however, is housed in the National Army Museum in Chelsea, London. Although much of the material is in storage at any given time, the Museum did stage a superb exhibition on the British soldier in southern Africa (1795–1914) to coincide with the centenary of the Anglo-Boer War. The catalogue to this exhibition, *Ashes and Blood*, edited by Peter B. Boyden, Alan J. Guy and Marion Harding (1999), contains excellent colour photographs of much of the Museum's southern African collection.

In South Africa, the National Museum of Military History in Johannesburg, which concentrates primarily on late 19th and 20th century conflicts, includes many exhibits and artefacts relating to the conflicts included in this book. The War Museum in Bloemfontein has extensive collections concerning the Anglo-Boer War. The MacGregor Museum in Kimberley has some material relating to the siege of this city in 1899–1900. The Talana Museum at Dundee – located in the heart of the 'battlefield region' in northern KwaZulu-Natal, not far from Majuba and on the very site of the first pitched battle of the Anglo-Boer War – has many displays relating to the 1881 and 1899–1902 conflicts in Natal, including weapons, items of Boer clothing and battlefield relics. The Siege Museum in Ladysmith has extensive and well-organised displays relating to the central role played by the town in the events of 1899–1900. The Block House Museum in Ladysmith, a private museum housed in a replica of an Anglo-Boer War period blockhouse, houses a fascinating array of memorabilia including Boer weapons. Anyone travelling throughout South Africa should also be aware that many small provincial museums have collections relating to local participation in the war.

The Anglo-Boer War involved a great deal of participation by troops from British colonies, and it should not be forgotten that material relating to the war can also be found in collections in Canada and Australia.

COLLECTING AND RE-ENACTMENT

There is a paucity of artefact material relating to Boer campaigns from 1876–1898. The small numbers of men involved, the almost total lack of collectible military insignia and the limited involvement of foreign military personnel means that few items have survived outside museums, and those that do emerge are seldom found outside South Africa. Even the 1880-81 campaign has produced few obvious fields for collecting. The campaign was not popular in Britain, and no campaign medal was awarded to commemorate it (although most of the British participants were entitled to medals for service prior to the war, either the Anglo-Zulu War or 2nd Afghan War). Despite their famous propensity to acquire souvenir items from almost any conflict, the lack of significant victories in the field meant that British troops were seldom in a position to recover relics of battle, and this explains their paucity on the market today.

A much more fertile area for collecting was the Anglo-Boer War of 1899–1902. This required an unprecedented military commitment from the British Empire, not merely in terms of regular British troops, but also of detachments from Dominions like Australia and Canada. The war involved thousands of combatants on both sides, and resulted in the extensive gathering of souvenirs – the main source for items emerging onto the market today. For those interested in collecting items relating to the British, mainstream militaria auction houses offer an almost constant stream of campaign medals, uniform items and period weapons. Items relating to the Boer forces are scarcer, but by no means impossible to find. Many of these were 'captured' by British troops during the war, and have been dispersed all over the world. They include Mauser rifles – sometimes with the original owner's names engraved on the butt, as these were highly prized as trophies – items of Boer clothing, occasionally Transvaal or OFS badges, Boer pipes and personal possessions, as well as contemporary battlefield debris. Such was the passion for retaining souvenirs during the period that shell fragments or bullet-heads picked up after 'near misses' were often eagerly seized upon.

The huge numbers of men involved meant that large numbers of letters and diaries from both sides have survived, while it is comparatively easy to obtain original photographic images from the period.

A separate collecting field in itself is the huge number of commemoratives produced in Britain during the war, including metal pin-buttons with pictures of famous generals for porcelain busts, decorated tea-caddies and money boxes. Anyone interested in exploring this field is advised to consult Pieter Oosthuizen's book *Boer War Memorabilia: The Collectors' Guide* (1987).

An interesting sub-category of Anglo-Boer War collectibles for those with a particular interest in the burgher perspective is prisoner-of-war art. Burghers captured in the field and shipped

A group of Free State commandos, armed with Mausers.

A montage of Boer leaders in the 1881 war. Note the style of clothing of the period, the bandoliers with loops for single rounds, and a preference for tall hats.

off to camps elsewhere in the Empire often whiled away their time by carving decorative items in wood or bone which were then sold for pocket money to local residents or to officers of the garrison. They are among the more personal and atmospheric items to find their way onto the market today.

Anyone seriously interested in collecting militaria from 19th century campaigns in South Africa is advised to consult the National Army Museum's catalogue to their *Ashes and Blood: The British Soldier in South Africa 1795–1914* (London 1999) exhibition, which includes a wealth of information on the sort of artefacts which survive from these wars.

NOTES

1 The Battle of Laing's Nek was the last time a British infantry battalion carried its Colours into action.
2 Both the Orange Free State (OFS) and SAR raised small professional artillery units, and the SAR a quasi-military police force. These units fall outside the scope of this title, however, as they were not part of the commando system.
3 The OFS mustered some 27,000 men at the start of the war.

GLOSSARY

Afrikaner descendant of the first Dutch and French settlers of southern Africa.
Agterryer African groom or servant serving with the commandos.
Biltong sun-dried meat.
Boer farmer, countryman.
Burgher citizen of the Boer republics, farmer.
Dominee minister of the Dutch reform Church.
Donga an erosion gully, usually dry except during the wet season.
Dorp a small rural town.
Drift a river crossing.
Impi Zulu term for an armed force.
Krygsraad council of war.
Laager defensive wagon circle or camp.
Landdrost district magistrate.

Mealies corn.
Neef 'nephew', term used by elderly Boer when addressing a younger man.
Oom 'uncle'; term of respect for an elderly Boer.
Penkoppe young Boers; a homely reference to frisky young animals just sprouting their horns.
Roinekke redneck, i.e. a British soldier.
Sjambok tough whip, traditionally made of hippo hide.
Uitlanders 'foreigners'; white immigrants, usually of British descent, who entered the SAR following the discovery of gold in 1885.
Veldt (veld) the open grass and scrubland of southern Africa.
Veldt-kornet; 'field cornet'; sub-commander within a commando.
Velskoen 'veldt shoes', home-made footwear.

BIBLIOGRAPHY

The following provide a vivid insight into commando life and other aspects of the period covered in this book:

Aylward, Alfred, *The Transvaal of Today*, London, 1878.

Bester, Ron, *Boer Rifles and Carbines of the Anglo-Boer War*, Johannesburg, 1995.

Carter, Thomas, *A Narrative of the Boer War*, London, 1883.

Castle, Ian, *Majuba: Hill of Destiny*, Cambridge, 1996.

De Wet, Christiaan, *Three Years War*, London, 1902.

Judd, Denis and Surridge, Keith, *The Boer War*, London, 2002.

Knight, Ian and Embleton, Gerry, *The Boer Wars (1: 1836–1896)*, Cambridge, 1997.

Knight, Ian and Embleton, Gerry, *The Boer Wars (2: 1896–1902)*, Cambridge, 1997.

Laband, John, *The Atlas of the Later Zulu Wars 1883–1888*, Pietermaritzburg, 2001.

Mossop, George, *Running the Gauntlet*, London, 1937.

Newnham-Davis, Lieutenant Colonel N., *The Transvaal Under the Queen*, London, 1900.

Pretorius, Fransjohan, *Life on Commando during the Anglo-Boer War 1899–1902*, Cape Town, 1999.

Rae, Rev. Colin, *Malaboch: Notes from My Diary on the Boer Campaign of 1894*, Cape Town, 1898.

Reitz, Denys, *Commando. A Boer Journal of the Boer War*, London, 1929.

Schikkerling, Roland, *Commando Courageous (A Boer Diary)*, Johannesburg, 1964.

Steele, Nick, *Take a Horse to the Wilderness*, Cape Town, 1971.

Warwick, Peter, *Black People in the South African War 1899–1902*, Cambridge, 1983.

COLOUR PLATES

A: JOHANNES DE BRUYN, C.1881

A suit of heavy-duty corduroy was a popular and practical choice for life in the field, although individual burghers dressed according to means and taste. Johannes is wearing home-made *velskoen* shoes of tanned animal hide, which were typical of the crafts produced by the self-reliant farming community. Single-shot breach-loading firearms – like this Martini-Henry rifle – were the most common form of armament, with ammunition carried in single rounds in a leather bandolier. Other weapons used in large quantities at this time were the Westley-Richards 'Monkey Tail' (1 and 1A), so-called because of the hooked lever which was hinged upwards to allow access to the breach, the 'Monkey Tail' was a percussion weapon which fired a paper-wrapped cartridge (2). Such cartridges were popular because they could be easily made at home on the farm. They were not as robust and resistant to damage as the metal cartridges fired by the Martini-Henry and the Westley-Richards 'falling-block' carbine (3), however. Since the burghers provided their own weapons, they purchased carbine or rifle versions of these guns according to preference. In this period, burgher clothes, even on campaign, were distinguished by a total lack of military insignia. Johannes would have carried little else on his person beyond a pocket knife – this one (4) is a type popular in the 1870s – a clay pipe (5) and tobacco. By the outbreak of the Anglo-Boer War in 1899, more sophisticated wooden pipes (6) had largely replaced the clay variety.

B: THE BATTLE OF LAING'S NEK, 28 FEBRUARY 1881

Burghers defend their trenches against an attack by the British 58th Regiment. The Boer trenches on this section of the battlefield had been placed so as to command about 80 yards of sloping ground in front of them; beyond this, the terrain dropped into a steep valley. The 58th advanced up the steep slope in column, then tried to deploy in line for a final assault as they emerged onto the open ground. At that range they were terribly exposed to the Boer fire, and suffered heavy casualties before abandoning the attack. This was the last occasion British troops carried Colours into action; their conspicuousness made the Colour bearers acutely vulnerable.

C: THE BATTLE OF TSHANENI, 5 JUNE 1884

The political settlement which followed the British invasion of Zululand in 1879 was deliberately divisive, and led to a protracted civil war. In 1884, the uSuthu (royalist) faction appealed to the SAR for support against the ascendant anti-royalist Mandlakazi faction. Although the SAR refused to intervene officially, a volunteer commando of about 100 men under Commandant Lukas Meyer, together with 20 volunteers from the German settlement at Luneburg, did join the fighting. On 5 June the combined Boer and royalist force was advancing along the banks of the Mkhuze river when the Mandlakazi ambushed them from the slopes of the Gaza and Tshaneni mountains. The royalists were initially driven back, but the burghers, following close behind, opened a devastating fire from the saddle, firing over their allies' heads. After stiff fighting, the Mandlakazi broke, and were ruthlessly chased from the field.

The battle marked a turning point in the Zulu Civil War, and demonstrated that modern breach-loading weapons had only bolstered the battlefield superiority of the horse and gun, which the Voortrekkers had demonstrated 50 years before.

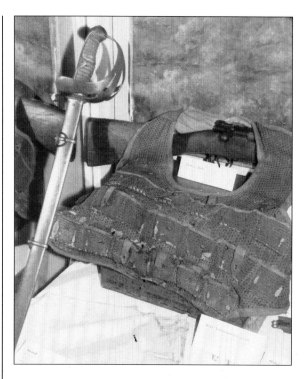

A webbing waistcoat, with sewn-in pockets to carry clips of Mauser ammunition. (Duke of Cornwall's Light Infantry Museum)

A Boer outpost outside Ladysmith. Note the shelter made from corrugated iron reinforced with sandbags. The man in the foreground is armed with a Portuguese-made single-shot Guedes rifle.

D: JOHANNES DE BRUYN ON THE EVE OF THE ANGLO-BOER WAR, 1899

Johannes is carrying the 1896 pattern 7mm Mauser rifle which was issued to the commandos in the months preceding the conflict. The Mauser was loaded by means of five-round clips, which were often carried in leather bandoliers such as the one Johannes is wearing. Nevertheless, as usual there was a great deal of variety in the way rounds were carried, including bandoliers of canvas webbing (1) or in specially designed waistcoats (2). Despite the obvious advantages of magazine rifles such as the Mauser, many burghers still entered the war with single-shot rifles like the old Martini-Henry, or the Portuguese Guedes (3). The Guedes was a curious mix of old and new styles, a single-shot weapon which fired a light 8mm cartridge, in contrast to the old .577/.450 of the Martini-Henry. A number of Guedes rifles were imported into South Africa in the mid-1890s, and some 6,000 had been bought by the two republics by the time the war began. Gradually, however, British attempts to restrict access for weapons to South Africa shut off the republics' source of resupply, and the commandos became increasingly dependent on captured British weapons, like the Lee-Metford (4) or Lee-Enfield. Both weapons largely equalled the performance levels of the Mauser, and captured British ammunition became more plentiful than Mauser rounds.

In 1899, many burghers adopted some sort of insignia reflecting their status as combatants – either cockade ribbons in the colours of the Free State or SAR (5), or metal hat badges bearing the Free State (6) or SAR (7) coat of arms. Some of these badges were apparently drawn from the stocks of the republics' small professional artillery units, while others were pressed out for the occasion.

E: A BOER COMMANDO IN THE FIELD DURING THE ANGLO-BOER WAR, 1899

Many burghers took their wagons with them to carry supplies and camp luxuries, and large numbers of cattle and sheep were driven 'on the hoof' as provisions. Most burghers carried little beyond their bandoliers on their person, and only a blanket, and perhaps a saddlebag, on their horses.

The African contribution to the Boer war effort, particularly at the beginning of the war, was significant. Burghers brought their farm workers with them to serve as *voorloopers* (wagon-drivers who walked alongside the ox-teams controlling them with long whips), *agterryers* (grooms) and general servants.

F: BURGHERS AT AN EVENING MEAL, EARLY 1900

The official food supply from the government to the commandos was erratic at the beginning of the war, and non-existent during the

A mounted attack launched under cover of a veldt fire at Vlakfontein in May 1901.

guerrilla phase. Burghers became increasingly dependent on typical farm produce – like the rusks shown here – and foraged vegetables. African labourers often collected firewood and cooked in the early stages of the war, but later the burghers were obliged to fend for themselves. The three-legged iron cooking pot was essential on commando, and if tin or enamel mugs were lost in the field they became prized treasures to be looted from the British Army. Many burghers took small coffee grinders and coffee pots with them on campaign, though these, together with plates and utensils, were often replaced at the expense of the British. When not actually engaged in battle, the burghers passed their evenings smoking, exchanging news, telling stories, playing simple musical instruments like the harmonica, or reading. Some rural burghers were illiterate, however, while many others felt the Bible was the only appropriate reading matter.

G: 'BITTER-ENDERS' LOOTING BRITISH WEAPONS AFTER A SUCCESSFUL ACTION, C.1901

By the time the guerrilla war was well advanced, the commandos were experiencing desperate shortages of almost everything. Clothing in particular had suffered, with most men wearing heavily patched items, and some dressed only in home-made clothes of leather or animal skins. By necessity, the burghers made extensive use of British clothing whenever they could obtain it. British prisoners were often asked to strip off their serviceable uniforms, which were appropriated by the Boers. This practise became so well known that British troops expected it, and while some were indignant at the process, most endured it philosophically or with good humour.

H: THE BATTLE OF HOLKRANS, 6 MAY 1902

As the guerrilla war progressed, some commandos were forced to forage extensively among African communities, a move which was increasingly resisted by those communities. The most serious incident of African retaliation took place at the very end of the war, near Vryheid in the area of the New Republic. A climate of resentment had existed between the burghers and some local groups dating back to the founding of the Republic in the aftermath of the Battle of Tshaneni in 1884. This was inflamed in early 1902 when the Vryheid commando, which was then operating from the farms of supporters outside the town, began to raid cattle and grain from the Zulu abaQulusi group. When the Zulus protested, *Veld-kornet* Potgeiter – who had a history of antagonism towards the abaQulusi Chief Sikhobhobho – dared them to respond. At dawn on the morning of 6 May a force of up to 1,000 abaQulusi surrounded the commando, which was camped around a stone cattle kraal on the lower slopes of a hill known as Holkrans. The burghers were largely asleep and were taken by surprise, and fled back up the hill with the Zulus in pursuit. The Boers rallied, however, and poured a heavy fire into the Zulus, forcing them to retreat. According to Zulu sources, the warriors then lay down in the long grass or among the bodies and were not spotted in the poor light. When the burghers emerged from their positions, a Zulu commander called out 'No! It is not yet finished!' and the Zulus rose up and overran the burghers. The battle was costly to both sides – 56 Boers were killed out of a total of 72, while the Zulus lost nearly 100 dead and wounded.

Commandants Jan Smuts (centre) and Mannie Maritz (with moustache and bow tie) photographed during the invasion of the Cape in late 1901. Although many commandos had a decidedly ragged appearance by this stage of the guerrilla war, Smuts encouraged a smart professional appearance in his men, many of whom are wearing captured British equipment and uniforms.

INDEX

References to illustrations are shown in **bold**. Plates are shown with page and caption locators in brackets.